# JOURNEY TO ONENESS

Enriching, Renewing and Reconciling
Marriage Relationships

Published by Life In Motion Resources™
Westerville, Ohio
http://www.lifeinmotionresources.com
Email: ron@lifeinmotionresources.com

ISBN-13: 9781517499440

ISBN-10: 1517499445

# Journey to Oneness

## Enriching, Renewing and Reconciling Marriage Relationships

### Dr. Ron Hitchcock

Marriage & Family Life Pastor

# Contents

# Acknowledgments

I want to thank my wife, Barbara, who daily walks out this Journey to Oneness with me. Our marriage truly made our dreams come true.

We are grateful for our daughter, Veronica, and son-in-law, Jeff, who have blessed us with two grandchildren, and our son, Ron Jr, who brings us joy.

Barbara and I had a dream that we would raise a family together and then have a chance to spoil our grand and, one day, great-grand-children with love and affection.

# Introduction

The Journey to Oneness was birthed out of a dramatic spiritual event in my life. I was praying for the teens in my church when the Lord spoke the following into my heart:

*I am going to frustrate the hand of youth ministry and drive it back to where it belongs, the home.*

These words changed everything about my life and ministry. My wife and I had made commitments to serve the church as career youth pastors and were enjoying the fruit of equipping teens to follow the Lord. We now understood that it was necessary to leave student ministries to establish a marriage and family life ministry in order to fulfill the mission of equipping couples and parents to disciple their children.

In the 1990's, marriage and family life ministries were under-developed in most local churches. Even though many of the parents that I worked with wanted to be actively engaged in the discipleship of their children, most resources approached discipleship as Bible memorization, service and prayer – the disciplines essential to Christian maturity. However, after years of pastoral interactions with families, I now know that children need relational models of discipleship in order to grow into mature believers who will reproduce healthy Christ-centered marriages and family life.

I developed the Journey to Oneness to equip parents to model Christ-centered relationships to their children. Couples who model a shared identity, friendship, validation and sacrificial love in their relationship will equip their children to do the same in their own marriages. I believe the best gift that parents can give their children is to model healthy marriage and parenting relationships in the home. Children will be able to reproduce these essential characteristics of relational maturity as they become spouses and parents.

*How to Use Journey to Oneness*

Throughout this book, you will read the stories of premarital and married couples who are addressing topics such as communication, conflict resolution, financial management or marital crisis. These stories represent real-life circumstances that will help couples to learn new ways of communicating and resolving conflict.

*Journey to Oneness* can be used individually or in group settings by premarital or married couples. The first half of the book will enrich *friendship* and *shared values* in premarital and marriage relationships. The second half of the book reveals how to *restore broken trust* and *reconcile crisis relationships.*

## What Should You Expect from the Journey?

The Journey to Oneness shows how relationships transition from individualism towards interdependence and a shared identity. Couples will discover that intimacy and commitment increase as they progress from one stage to the next.

- *Premarital couples* will find that the Journey to Oneness empowers them to establish healthy boundaries that promote mutuality in friendships and validation of each other's values. Dating couples are responsible to encourage each other's pursuit of their dreams and goals. Couples in the friendship/dating stage are not a "we" but two friends who are learning to have each other's best interest in mind.
- *Married couples* will be revisiting or reinvesting in one or more of the stages of the Journey to Oneness that are underdeveloped in order to cultivate the characteristics of friendship or shared values in their relationship.

At times, couples will prioritize their parenting responsibilities, careers or hobbies above their friendship with each other. When this happens, couples feel disconnected, even though they are committed to their marriage and family life. Couples will be able to rekindle their friendship by reinvesting in areas of communication, conflict resolution or sexual intimacy.

• The Journey to Oneness offers resources and practical application that allow couples to establish the foundational pieces of friendship and shared values. For some couples, values were underdeveloped while others began their marriage without a strong friendship.

## The Life In Motion Resources™ Research Project

For my doctoral dissertation, I gathered data in order to find correlations between friendship and shared values with couple satisfaction in premarital and married couples. The results of my research and experiences as a Marriage & Family Life Pastor over the last twenty years support and establish the importance of shared values as a basis for the success of long-term marriage relationships.

In relationships that report couple satisfaction, partners can trust their boy/girlfriend, fiancé or spouse to make decisions and choices that are consistent with each other's values. You can have many friends who do not share your values, but you would not want to marry any of them. Here is an overview of the resources that are available for this purpose.

### Life In Motion Resources™

In order to enrich couple satisfaction in dating, engaged and marriage relationships, Life In Motion Resources™ is offering a free Relationships Growth Plan for my readers. The Life In Motion Relationships Inventory (LIMRI) measures friendship, shared values and couple satisfaction in dating, engaged and married relationships. You can find out more about the LIMRI at www.lifeinmotionresources.com. To receive the free inventory, go to www.limri.org/relationships.

The LIMRI is an online assessment tool that churches, counselors and Christian organizations can utilize to enrich the relationships of their members, clients, staff, leadership, or employees. Couples answer demographic questions that generate personalized inventories for dating, engaged or married couples. The LIMRI is a values-based inventory that uses Scriptures, biblical principles and healthy relationship practices to increase couple satisfaction in couple and parenting relationships.

The relationship targets of the LIMRI include: communication, conflict resolution, spiritual life, shared spiritual life, finances, personality, respect, emotional honesty, and relationship satisfaction. Parenting targets include: parenting and parenting our children targets. Couples with children from former relationships receive parenting his/her children targets. These targets are available for engaged and married couples. The future sexual relationship target is exclusive to engaged couples. Only married couples receive the sexual relationship target.

The LIMRI is a reliable and valid instrument that measures friendship and shared values. These characteristics have strong correlations to couple satisfaction. The LIMRI generates personalized worksheets and growth plans that allow couples to enrich friendship and shared values in their relationships.

## LIMRI Worksheets

Each worksheet and growth plan includes Scriptures, principles, discussion questions and practical applications. These resources offer couples spiritual and practical applications that are essential for establishing shared values and healthy boundaries in their relationships with spouses and children.

The worksheets are modeled after an ancient Christian discipline, *Lectio Divina*. This traditional Benedictine practice of Scripture reading, meditation and prayer is intended to promote communion with God and to increase the knowledge of God's Word. The practice of *Lectio Divina* does not treat Scripture as texts to be studied, but as the Living Word of God (Wikipedia, 2015).

Couples meditate on the Scriptures, principles, discussion questions and practical applications before answering the questions in each section of the worksheets. The man and woman complete the first half of the worksheet individually and then share their answers with each other. Spiritual conversations happen naturally as couples share insights from their worksheets in response to the Scriptures, principles, discussion questions and practical applications.

Couples also receive insight on how to pray for each other as they discuss key words from the Scriptures, practical applications or principles that were significant to them. One spouse may say: "I was impressed with the idea of being watchful and devoted in our prayer life. I believe the Lord is showing me that I need to be attentive to this area of our relationship." His/her spouse will then know how to pray for them: "Lord, help my husband/wife to be diligent in being watchful and devoted to his/her prayer life."

Growth plans and worksheets allow couples to gain new insights and relational skills in areas where improvement is needed in boy-to-girlfriend, fiancé-to-fiancée and spouse-to-spouse relationships.

The man and woman are given separate four-digit pin numbers to ensure privacy. Neither the man nor the woman can see the other's answers or conversations with their coaches as they complete the first half of the worksheet. The top section of each worksheet offers spiritual and practical insights that couples use to strengthen and enrich areas of their relationships.

The LIMRI statements are personalized as couples identify their relationship status in the demographic section. Couples selecting "dating" will generate boy/girlfriend statements such as "My boy/girlfriend is a good listener". Engaged couples will generate statements such as "My fiancé is a good listener", and married couples will generate statements such as "My spouse is a good listener". The worksheets and growth plans are generated as couples agree or disagree with 150 statements such as:

- I am a good listener – my spouse is a good listener
- I resolve conflicts quickly – my spouse resolves conflicts quickly
- I forgive quickly – my spouse forgives quickly
- I ask my spouse to pray with me – my spouse asks me to pray with him/her

In the Appendices at the end of this book, you will find examples of worksheets and growth plans that allow couples to celebrate their strengths and to enrich areas of their relationships that need to improve. You will also find assessments that allow anyone who is dating, engaged or married to determine how their relationship measures up against the characteristics and values that correlate to couple satisfaction in the different stages of relationships. These assessments are titled: Engaged/Seriously Dating Couple's, and Married Couple's Assessments.

Part I

# Journey to Oneness

# CHAPTER ONE

# Before You Begin the Journey

The Journey to Oneness brings a fresh and new approach to relationships. The following topics will help couples experience the best of dating, engaged or married relationships. I hope that couples will benefit from the unlimited potential of Christ-centered relationships.

## The Marionette Myth

I firmly believe that one of the greatest threats to healthy premarital relationships is what I call the Marionette Myth. This is the belief that all things are predetermined for us. Many premarital couples have asked me:

1. "Am I to wait until the Lord speaks or shows me a sign as to whom I should date?"
2. "Do I date as many people as it takes until I find the right person to marry?"

I want to say clearly to both of these questions: yes, and no! Too often I have observed that the goal of premarital relationships becomes a search for "the one" rather than preparing to be "the one" (gift) that God desires to give to their future spouse.

The Marionette Myth puts God in the position of serving us instead of us following him. Relationships are holy, and we are more than actors playing out the wishes of a puppet master within a cosmic puppet show entitled, *Find Your Spouse*. Couples who expect God to somehow orchestrate their relationships will often abdicate their responsibilities to develop the values that form a shared identity and vibrant marriage.

Another extreme position of the Marionette Myth occurs when someone comes up to you and says: "God has told me to marry you." Decisions like this should never be trusted to another person's ability to hear from God on your behalf. Everyone is responsible for his or her own decisions.

Many couples will short circuit the premarital process, believing that the Marionette Myth predetermines who they should marry. These couples will move onto a marriage pathway before they have fully established the characteristics of Identity, Friendship, Committed Dating and Engagement. Couples who bypass *any* of these stages will discover that key elements of a vibrant relationship are missing after three to five years of married life.

### Are Relationships Predestined or Pretentious?

The pivotal event in my life happened in 1977, when I made the decision to move from California to Montana. My grandfather had passed away unexpectedly during my senior year of high school. The previous year, I had made plans to live with my grandparents and attend the University of Montana, but his unexpected death set in motion a series of events that rushed my time line to leave California. I checked out of my high school and transferred to a school in the Bitterroot Valley in order to care for my widowed grandmother.

This crisis event also set in motion a series of choices that led to a relationship with my future wife. Most likely, I would have never met my future wife if my time line had not been moved up.

My new plans included providing care for my grandmother and concentrating on a college degree, but these plans quickly changed

– for the better. I was living in a different state, away from my immediate family and friends, and attending a new high school in this small town identified by a single flashing yellow light as you drove down the highway. One day, as I was riding my motorcycle down Main Street, I pulled up to two girls. I stopped next to them and asked who would be willing to take a ride to the hardware store because I needed someone to hold up my motorcycle while I went inside. (You could say I asked her to be my kickstand.) Barbara volunteered, and the rest is history. (My motorcycle actually didn't have a kickstand.)

The Marionette Myth will challenge us to think about the way life works:

- Does God pull us in and out of relationships, states, careers, or Christian ministries?
- Or are we responsible to ask him to bless our choice of relationships, careers and ministries?

I say yes to both of these questions, but I lean more in the direction of the latter question when I explain how things happen in our lives. I believe that, by submitting our choices, relationships and dreams to God, we acknowledge that he has plans and purposes in all areas of our lives. His wisdom, provision, admonitions and blessings guide us to make the best decisions toward faith-filled relationships. We can never predict what seemingly small circumstances or choices may impact our future in positive or negative ways. The important thing is to invite God into every relationship, circumstance and decision over your lifetime. God is not surprised by our choices, whether good or bad. He knows every outcome. Yet He redeems every decision for his glory and our growth as his son/daughter as we thank him for every positive outcome and repent for every poor decision (Romans 8:28–29).

Couples do not just appear before each other at a predetermined time, as if they were waiting for a cue from a stage manager to begin Scene Two of Act One in a marionette's puppet show. God is not limited to a specific time line for our lives. There is no prewritten script that says God must have Ron turn the corner at 3.45 p.m. and have Barbara walking down Main Street at 3.44 p.m. so that he will stop and ask her for a ride on his motorcycle. After thirty-six years of marriage, I believe that Barbara is God's blessing and messenger of grace and mercy to me. And I know that our relationship is not based solely on our ability to respond to providence that determines everything for us in advance. We must work at our marriage in order to add blessings and eliminate self-centered attitudes and behavior. Couples must choose to be gifts to each other.

I have talked with many single adults who have tapped out of the dating scene for various reasons and taken a position of letting God do the choosing for them. The belief that God will match you with his choice of a spouse sounds wonderful and spiritual. Who is in a better position to match anyone up with their future spouse than the Creator of the universe? No longer is anyone required to wrestle with the questions of who and when to marry. Sounds great, right? Not really.

Let's play out this scenario to an extreme by asking if it would be important to meet your spouse before the wedding day, since God is going to create a spouse exclusively for you. All you would have to do is pray about the day, hour and location of your wedding and just show up at church. Wait a second! You don't like that idea? Why not? Couples must decide which strategy they will follow when choosing a future spouse.

Strategy #1:   God chooses my spouse for me.
Strategy #2:   I am solely responsible for my choice of a future spouse.
Strategy #3:   Both statements are true.

Many generations of Christians have struggled with an embedded belief that there is only one person who is predestined to be your spouse.

*I truly believe in a specific man or woman being "the one"
in your life. He or she is "the one" that you marry.*

While it is true that God knows the name of your spouse and the date, time, and location of your wedding day, and that he is not surprised or taken back by whom you choose as a spouse, it is also true that each person is responsible to pray and submit their relationship to God before they commit to marriage.

Strategy #3 places the responsibility on each person to become the gift that God wants them to be for their future spouse. Couples who focus on being gifts to one another will be on their way to vibrant, Christ-centered marriages.

Another negative outcome associated with abdicating your choice of a spouse to God sounds like this: "Since God brought us together, he will take care of any problems that we will face in our marriage." Couples who adopt this philosophy will ignore their individual responsibilities to develop their communication, conflict resolution and shared values, because God is responsible to fix all their marriage problems. This is faulty thinking, plain and simple.

### Looking for Romance or Love?

I have listened to many couples tell their stories of how God brought them together. I commonly hear:

- "We ran into each other four times in one day."
- "I prayed that he would start a conversation with me at church, and he did."
- "I want to serve on the mission field, so I asked God to bring someone into my life who wants to be a missionary."
- "I write worship songs and play the guitar. I am asking God to bless me with a spouse who will sing my songs."

These stories are fun and romantic to hear as I help couples complete the Journey to Oneness but, unfortunately, some of these couples are back in my office two years later asking me: "Why would God do this to me?" I have learned that what they are really asking is: "If God intended this person to be a blessing in my life, why would he/she make things so difficult for me?"

The missionary couple discovered that their spouse felt called to different people groups, while the songwriter realized that his spouse disliked those songs. This happens because, too often, couples carry the romance of faith into their relationships but forgo the responsibility to develop relationships based on friendships and shared values. Romance is amazing, but it does not sustain a relationship with God nor with our spouse. Couples need to develop values as well as nurture their romance.

A pretentious mindset has no factual basis on which to stand, only assumptions. And these assumptions can exaggerate one's own importance. The belief that every person you choose to date represents God's best for you is not grounded in reality. Only God knows whether your boy/girlfriend, fiancé or spouse's choices will bring blessings or discipline into your life. Couples must be willing to do the hard work of establishing the values in each stage of the Journey to Oneness in order to give them the best opportunity to develop a healthy relationship.

I firmly believe that, when couples submit their relationship to God, they will receive confirmation of whether to continue or break off premarital relationships. Dozens of spouses have told me, following a crisis in their marriage, that God had told them not to marry their spouse. Some of these couples report that God warned them on their walk down the aisle on their wedding day. But because they wanted to get married so badly and start a family, they ignored his words. It breaks my heart when spouses tell me these types of stories.

There is a fine line between thinking about relationships as being predestined and being gripped by the fear of being alone. This can motivate couples to marry someone even when they have doubts about their character or commitment to Jesus.

*Are You Looking for "the One"? Or Are You Becoming "the One"?*

I do not believe that God is a cosmic matchmaker. He empowers men and women to choose future spouses and develop loving, faithful and rewarding relationships. Every person is responsible to invest the proper amount of time and attention required to form healthy relationships. Not all friendships develop into committed relationships; not all committed relationships will transition into engagements, and not all engagements culminate in marriage. Most dating relationships are short-lived, but these relationships help you to identify the personal characteristics and values that are nonnegotiable in a future spouse.

All relationships have learning curves. God's kingdom is unlike any human institution because it is based on relationships. The kingdom of God does not have anything to do with positon, authority, talent, culture or wealth. Marriage works in the same way. God expresses his kingdom in marriage as a unique expression of covenant relationships, and couples must learn how to develop a shared identity based on their faith in Christ Jesus.

Our relationship with Jesus begins with confession, repentance and receiving forgiveness of our sins. You cannot form a shared identity with someone who is not a follower of Jesus or is unwilling to confess, repent of their sins and seek or extend forgiveness when needed. Marriage relationships form their identity out of their commitment to faith, confession, repentance and forgiveness.

Men and women who struggle to develop and maintain healthy dating relationships may one day struggle to maintain friendship with their spouse. Marriage is not something that people are simply born to do well. A great marriage is based on the characteristics of friendship, but includes the shared values of confession, repentance, and forgiveness, the foundational values in the kingdom of God. A recent convert would quickly become frustrated with the Christian life without an understanding of how confession, repentance and forgiveness work in the kingdom of God. The same is true for dating, engaged and marriage relationships.

## Why Do Values Matter?

*Guarding Your Relationship from Your Past*

Premarital education and marriage coaching will help couples to figure out if any of their conflicts are being triggered by the negative effects of their family of origin. Someone who has experienced physical, emotional, verbal or sexual abuse, abandonment, divorce or drug/alcohol abuse as a child, often discovers that relationships trigger broken trust and abusive behaviors from their past.

> *Victims of abuse desperately want their relationship to create an oasis from all the chaos that they experienced during their childhood or in past relationships.*

The person who is in a relationship with a survivor of abuse is not responsible for something that they had no part in, but they may unknowingly trigger something from the abused person's past. Couples with these backgrounds often need professional help to keep both partners from having unrealistic expectations of their relationship. Survivors of abuse will need to guide their boy/girlfriend, fiancé or spouse through the emotional triggers resulting from these traumatic events.

> *A couple may be experiencing a great weekend when, all of a sudden, one word or look sends the wounded person reeling with confusion or anger.*

God is the healer of each person's past trauma. No one should feel as if they are damaged goods or destined to a life of brokenness. One of the ways you can become a gift to your spouse is to seek healing and restoration of your life before entering marriage. If you are currently married and are struggling with past trauma, be sure to seek healing through your local church or Christian counseling. God will honor every act of faith and obedience in order to bring wholeness into the marriage relationship.

## Culture of Relationships

It is critical for pastors to prepare their congregations to understand how different marriage looks in the New Millennium, with up to two-thirds of first marriages being preceded by cohabitation. This trend is reinforced by higher unemployment, educational expenses and declining confidence in career stability.

I have also observed many couples trying to avoid the legal responsibilities of marriage laws. Marriage contracts require people to agree to share everything, including debt, assets and parenting responsibilities. Becoming legally responsible for someone else's behavior and choices is perceived as a daunting responsibility.

I see a comparison between cohabiting couples and silent partners in a business relationship. The silent partner receives benefits or shares in the profits, but their name and other assets are protected against the losses of the business. I believe that cohabiting relationships are like silent partnerships. Traditionally, marriage has been defined as an "all-in" proposition, where couples must be willing to choose against all other possible romantic, intimate or emotionally fulfilling relationships.

Education is one of the issues affecting marriages. Couples who have a college education are more likely to marry than couples with high school diplomas (BEFORE IT'S NEWS, 2013). The number of marriages fell from 2.197 million to 2.080 million between 2007 and 2009 (Loehrke, 2013). Even though these trends can be disheartening, 88% of people surveyed in the U.S. agree that couples who marry should make lifelong commitments to each other. The children of divorce desire more stability in their relationships than their parents were able to maintain. These respondents also feel that

American culture would be better off if divorces were harder to attain (Glenn, 2005).

The suspicion that unmarried couples have about marital success has become known as "capstone marriage". A capstone marriage describes how cohabiting couples think about marriage. Nearly 50% of cohabiting couples marry after completing their education, securing work in his/her career field and having children (Cherlin, 2010).

*At one time, marriage was viewed as the foundation stone on which young couples built their family and life together.*

Capstone marriages have become symbols of successful lives that validate their choices, rather than two people beginning a journey of faith.

I am not critical of couples who follow this cultural trend. Many young adults have lost two generations of marriages in their families since the passing of no-fault divorce legislation in 1969. Today's young adults not only experienced divorce of parents, but also of grandparents and aunts and uncles. Unfortunately, capstone marriages do not lead to more long-term marriages.

The Journey to Oneness will help young adults to develop relationship skills and find hope to offset their concerns that their marriages will be different to and stronger than those of their families of origin.

## Comparing Cultural Values to Biblical Values for Relationships

Relationships are big business in the United States. Web-based corporations spend millions of dollars on advertisements, promising to help single adults find future spouses. These messages communicate that experts and science are needed to discover your future spouse, and that attraction and compatibility are vital elements of long-term relationships.

Millions of single adults sign up with web-based dating businesses, hoping that one of the thousands of clients might become their soul mate. Many married couples hear these dating commercials and wonder if their relationship has any chance of achieving couple satisfaction because they were not paired through scientific algorithms. Attraction and compatibility have some value in relationships, but shared values are the glue of long-term marriages.

Web-based dating sites claim that up to *23 million* single adults utilize their services. My concern is this belief that attraction and compatibility alone are the definitive factors in long-term relationships. Based on my pastoral interactions with couples over the past twenty years, this misguided conclusion misses the real glue of long-term relationships, which is solidly based on the couple's shared values.

Attraction can be based on physical looks, age, body type, careers, education, personality, or other characteristics. Compatibility is based on mutuality of interests, such as sports, music, performing arts, hiking, quality of life (health or exercise) or hobbies. Even though attraction and compatibility can create feelings of excitement and appealing connections, they have a limited capacity to keep couples together.

*Long-term relationships thrive when couples have formed shared values in areas such as faith, finances, shared spiritual life, parenting, respect and responsibility. These values promote honor, trust and validation in dating, engaged, and marriage relationships.*

In the following chapters, we will see how these values underscore every stage of the Journey to Oneness.

# CHAPTER TWO

# The Journey to Oneness Model

Not all journeys begin with a destination in mind. But one thing is sure, all endings look different from their beginning. Travelers or adventures desire to arrive at their destinations in order to celebrate an ending of a journey. For some, the end of a journey will be the beginning of another or a return to where it all began. However, the journey of a relationship has different goals or outcomes than those of an explorer or adventurer.

Relationships do not begin in order to end. Unfortunately, too many premarital couples see marriage as an ending of superficial commitments by embracing the ultimate expression of devotion. Weddings do not have magical powers that make someone a mature or even a healthy spouse. Spouses must be committed to grow in their devotion, communication, conflict resolution, and shared identity over the lifetime of their marriage.

Too many couples lose their way quickly after their wedding day, because they did not understand how the beginning of their marriage and the ending of their singleness are uniquely tied together. All premarital relationships are underdeveloped in their friendships and shared values because they have not been measured under the weight of covenant love. Most couples will feel as if they can let go of their beginnings and forge a new journey following their wedding day.

Some couples began their relationship:

- Thinking that his/her girl/boyfriend needed them for validation, protection or provision.
- Feeling pressured to get married by a certain age in order to avoid loneliness.
- Feeling that God wanted them to marry a specific person, even if they were not attracted to them.

Couples must overcome these types of beginning in order to form mutuality and interdependence in their marriage relationship.

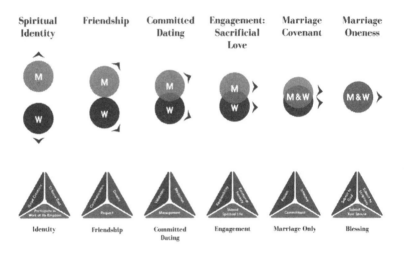

**The Journey to Oneness Model: The Six Stages**

The diagram above identifies the six stages of relationships, also known as the Journey to Oneness. These stages include:

1. *Spiritual Identity* – Men and women belong to God alone. In order to grow in their Spiritual Identity, they must discover what the Bible says about who they are and why they exist.
2. *Friendship* is a mutual agreement between two people who are committed to develop respect and uplifting communication, and encourage each other's dreams.

3. *Committed Dating (Validation)* addresses the need for validation in the relationship. Validation means to accept and celebrate someone for who they are. Couples in the Committed Dating stage need to validate each other as unique creations of God, uniquely responsible to glorify God through their gifts and talents as ambassadors of grace and mercy in the world.

4. *Engagement (Sacrificial Love)* means loving someone more than your own life. Men and women must be sure that their fiancé is mature enough to love them in this way.

5. *Marriage Covenant (One Flesh)* – God makes couples to be one, but not the same. The "joining" of a man and woman in holy matrimony means to "glue [them] together" or "keep [them] close".

6. *Marriage Oneness (Blessing)* – God will not withhold his wisdom and blessings from couples who seek him together. A person who submits to God and the Scriptures receives heavenly blessings and her/his spouse becomes a recipient of God's favor, kindness and encouragement.

Each of the six stages in the diagram on page 26 has three characteristics, as seen in the diagram below.

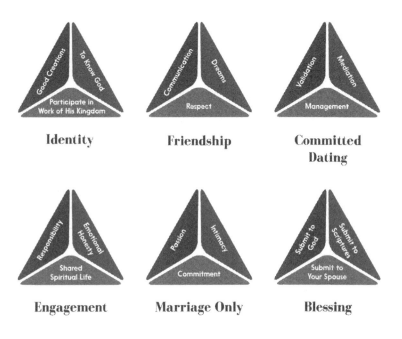

**Identity**          **Friendship**          **Committed Dating**

**Engagement**          **Marriage Only**          **Blessing**

**Characteristics of the Six Stages**

These characteristics equip couples to enrich the friendship, shared values and couple satisfaction in their relationship. We will look closely at each of the stages and its corresponding characteristics in the following chapters.

# CHAPTER THREE

# Spiritual Identity and Friendship

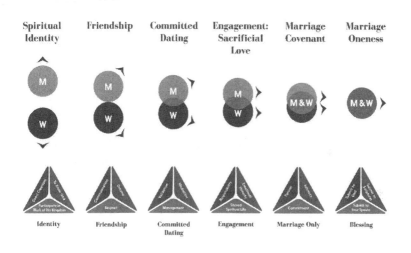

The Journey to Oneness Model

As we saw in the diagram on page 26, each of the six stages in the Journey to Oneness has three characteristics that equip couples to enrich the friendship and shared values and experience couple satisfaction in their relationships. Stage I is Identity.

## Spiritual Identity

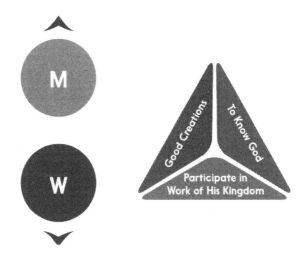

**Stage I: Identity**

The circles and arrows represent the Spiritual Identity of the man and woman. Each person is a unique, unrepeatable, miracle of God created with a divine purpose and spiritual identity. The distance between the circles is representative of each person's unique identity. Men and women belong to God alone. In order to grow in their Spiritual Identity, they must discover what the Bible says about who they are and why they exist (John 10:29; 13:33). For example, the top circle represents husbands while the bottom circle represents wives. Each person is created to know and experience God. Their identities are independent of each other, yet they share a unique identity with God.

The first stage of the Journey to Oneness seeks to identify the formational truths about each person's individual identity before God:

- We are a good creation (Genesis 1:27).
- God knows us and is aware of our history, circumstances and choices (Romans 5:8).
- God empowers us to participate in the work of his kingdom (Jeremiah 1:5).

## A Good Creation

Each person was created as a beautiful expression of the goodness of Almighty God. Through our faith in Christ, we are filled with his presence to serve as a testament to his love and devotion. We are his children and will live with him throughout eternity.

## To Know God

The Bible records the relationship that God has forged with humankind through his Son, Jesus. As believers, we are now invited to know him and experience his presence. He is able to sustain us in difficult times and empower us to overcome the spiritual attacks of the kingdom of darkness.

- 1 John 4:7: Everyone who loves is born of God.
- Romans 1:20: Creation reveals God's character and glory.
- 1 Peter 5:7: God cares for you.

## Participate in the Work of His Kingdom

Husbands and wives are created to be priests in God's kingdom (1 Peter 2:5). As priests, they are created to be participants, not spectators, in his divine plan of reconciliation. The blessings, power and love of God can be experienced as they share these attributes with others. We will never fully understand the depth of the words that were spoken to Jeremiah:

> *"Before I formed you in the womb I knew you;*
> *Before you were born I sanctified you;*
> *I ordained you a prophet to the nations." (Jeremiah 1:5 NKJV)*

This passage assures us that – before we are born into the physical world – God knows us, and he prepares us to communicate his Word and demonstrate love, grace and justice in the world.

## Who Is My Partner/Spouse?

I am asking premarital and married couples to reconsider how they think about relationships. At this point in the book, it makes no difference if you are married or single. In order to capture all that marriage means, couples need to reexamine what they believe about each other.

- Do you see one another as two human beings searching for significance and security, or as followers of Jesus who have amazing destinies (2 Corinthians 5:17)?
- Do you celebrate his/her identity as a redeemed and transformed follower of Jesus, or do you see them with their flaws and/or weaknesses as damaged goods?

The perception of your fiancé or spouse means everything. Many single adults wrestle with the following questions:

- "Who is the person God wants me to marry?"
- "How do I find him or her?"

Choosing a spouse is one of the most important decision in someone's life because they will have the greatest influence on their dreams and goals. This is why churches need to include information on how to choose a future spouse in its discipleship process of all young adults.

Perhaps the best way to describe discipleship is by dividing the word in half, "disciple" and "ship".

- "Disciples" are men, women and children who confess that Jesus is Lord and Savior of their lives.
- "Ships" represent events, circumstances, decisions, talents and relationships that must be submitted to God and his Word. These ships carry us along in our journey of faith. God uses all of these "ships" and all possible outcomes – whether positive or negative – to form us into mature disciples.

Dating relationships are like "ships" that create unique growth opportunities for men and women. These relationships allow couples to discover things about themselves that could not be discovered in other ways.

The popularity of online dating services shows that many young adults have given up on traditional ways of meeting someone. I have spoken with many frustrated singles who say: "I've done my best and nothing has worked out. So I'm just going to wait until God tells me who I should marry." Single adults may have joined numerous online relationships services, attended premarital classes and exhausted opportunities at their churches without finding a future spouse.

My experiences as a pastor over the last ten years show that many young adults abandon relationships too early, because they become frustrated with how long it takes to develop a committed relationship. Many singles in their late twenties are only beginning to think about engaging in committed relationships.

*Someone who desires marriage before age twenty-seven will find fewer potential spouses ready to make a similar commitment.*

I believe these struggles stem from the absence of healthy models of marriage in their childhood. The United States has the highest rates of divorce and father absence in the world (Maxwell, 2004). These negative family experiences often lead young adults to seek alternatives to marriage, such as cohabiting. Statistically, cohabiting couples are less likely than noncohabiting couples to experience lifelong marriage. In many cases, cohabiting before marriage makes things worse after the wedding.

## Friendship

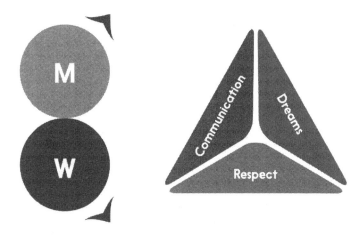

**Stage II: Friendship**

Friendship is the trailhead for every relationship that will one day lead to a committed relationship. As the circles and arrows in the Friendship stage begin to move closer to each other, something dramatic starts to happen. When two people spend more time together, they naturally begin to think less like independents and more like a couple. The relationship enriches each person's identity as they begin to form a significant friendship.

Friendship is a mutual agreement between two people who are committed to develop mutuality, respect and communication, and encourage each other's dreams. The Friendship stage lets couples know what is expected of them as a friend and allows them to prioritize these characteristics. Couples who neglect these key elements of friendship in their premarital relationship may struggle to maintain a growing friendship with each other following their wedding.

The best way to define friendship is to divide the word in half: "friend" and "ship". "Friend" identifies the two people who will be sharing common experiences over an undetermined length of time.

"Ship" describes shared experiences that form deeper levels of commitment to each other.

## Transitioning into a Dating Relationship

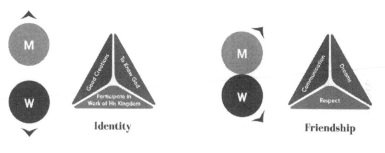

Identity                    Friendship

**First Transition**

The diagram above shows the transition from Identity to Friendship/dating. The Friendship stage shows the circles moving closer to each other and the arrows bending inward. In order to make the transition from individuals to couples, each person must be confident in their personal identity. A person without a mature spiritual identity will expect her/his boy/girlfriend to make them feel secure and significant rather than each person having their needs met by Christ Jesus.

*Many relationships fail when one person abandons*
*their spiritual identity.*

Couples can celebrate each other's identity, but they cannot be the source of significance and security for one another. A mature identity will help couples to overcome difficult seasons of life and avoid independent or codependent behaviors from taking root in their relationship.

*New Beginnings*

In the following story, we will discover how Jake and Carol began their friendship.

*Jake and Carol first met at an outdoor party hosted by a couple in their church. Jake arrived early, looking forward to meeting new people. Suddenly, in walked Carol. His eyes locked onto her and his heart rate began to rise.*

*Jake explained, "It was as if my heart stopped beating for a moment and then it thumped like someone plucked the lowest note on a bass guitar."*

*Their eyes met for a moment as she looked over the many faces on the outdoor deck.*

*When Jake saw Carol, everything inside of him yelled, "I want to meet that woman!" Carol saw Jake and thought, "Cute guy," but she quickly averted her eyes and began to talk with other guests. And so it went! Jake saw the woman of his dreams, but Carol was slow on the draw.*

*No matter, Jake made his way over to her and struck up a conversation. The conversation went well, and by the end of the evening, they decided to get a cup of coffee on their way home.*

*They started seeing each other weekly and quickly progressed into multiple connections per week.*

When Carol agreed to meet for coffee, Stage II (Friendship) of the Journey to Oneness began to take shape. This is the place where couples share their likes and dislikes about music, people, jobs, food, etc.

After a few months of dating, couples should invite each other into their personal friendships and family relationships. These additional contacts allow couples to receive feedback from people they trust in regard to how their boy/girlfriend treats them. In this stage, a couple should discuss their dreams and goals with each other to ensure that their dating partner shows interest in and is positive about these future plans.

## Communication – Words of Friendship

Communication is normally a relational strength between dating and engaged couples, while a lack of communication is usually at the heart of a crisis marriage. Communication styles that are affirming and respectful, such as: "I believe in you" or: "I will always believe the best about you" allow couples to develop deeper levels of intimacy and trust in their relationship.

- Write down some words or phrases that describe the friendship with your boy/girlfriend, fiancé or spouse.

*How Family of Origin Impacts Communication Styles*

*Jake and Carol had been dating for a few months when they encountered their first big conflict. She had noticed that Jake rarely shared his personal opinions with her. Carol really enjoyed the way he would listen as she expressed her opinions on subjects such as politics and community issues. She frequently asked Jake for his input on these subjects, yet he rarely expressed an opinion.*

*Whenever Carol pressed him for a response, he quickly changed the subject. After many frustrated conversations, Carol couldn't take it any longer.*

*"Don't you care about these important issues?" she asked.*

*Jake shot back, "I care, but your opinions are not the only way to look at these issues."*

*Jake felt that Carol expected him to agree with her comments. But Carol never wanted him to interpret her opinions as anything more than conversation starters.*

Jake grew up in a household where strong opinions usually ended up in heated arguments. He learned quickly that personal opinions were best kept private. Carol grew up with a completely different family system that treated everyone's opinions with openness and respect.

She wanted the same level of openness from Jake that she had developed with her mother.

Carol and her mother were able to talk about everything as she was growing up. Personal opinions were validated, even when they did not agree with each other. As a result, Carol expected Jake to express his personal opinions without fear of offending her. Unfortunately, he was unable to respond in kind because of his cautious attitude toward conflict that was modeled in his family of origin.

## Adjustments that Enhance Communication

Jake and Carol need to adjust their communication styles in order to experience enjoyable conversations. Jake needs to be willing to discuss topics that motivate Carol, even though he feels uninformed or indifferent about politics or community issues. She needs him to be a sounding board for her opinions and concerns. Carol needs to be sensitive to how often she engages him in these type of conversations.

Carol was naturally inclined to be more open when discussing controversial topics and she was not threatened when talking to others who were more knowledgeable than her. But Jake felt threatened when discussing unfamiliar topics. Carol had a highly developed emotional honesty. But Jake was not at the same place.

In order for couples to overcome communication struggles, they must avoid judging an opinion that is different from their own. Couples must allow each other to express opinions without feeling judged or competing against one another. A difference in opinion does not make someone right or wrong, nor does it make anyone good or bad. Different only means different.

## Discussion Questions

1. Why does the communication between Jake and Carol become stalled? In what ways do your conversations stall out in your relationship?

2. What can Carol do to make Jake more interested in talking with

her? What can you do to show that you are interested in subjects that your boy/girlfriend, fiancé or spouse cares about?

3. What can Jake do to communicate more effectively with Carol? What could you do to communicate more effectively in your relationship?

## Friendship Is More than Attraction and Compatibility

In this chapter, the focus has been on a couple's transition between the Spiritual Identity and Friendship stages. Friendship is a key element of each stage of the Journey to Oneness.

Married couples need more than what attraction and compatibility can offer them because the one constant in life is change. People change their habits, hobbies, beliefs and preferences throughout their lifetime. Couples will find that compatibility is greatly influenced as they transition from one life stage to the next:

- Young adulthood: 18–33 years
- Adulthood: 34–45 years
- Midlife: 45–63 years
- Senior years: 64 years and up

These life stages are also influenced by parenting young children or adolescents, or empty-nesting.

Couples are surprised at how quickly their relationship begins to regress when attraction and compatibility are its dominant characteristics. Compatibility is often challenged in the transitions between the life stages. Couples rarely notice the decline in their friendship from one life stage to the next because it is a slow process, like erosion. Erosion occurs whenever the banks of a river are missing trees, vegetation and boulders. Shared values have the same effect on relationships. Couples who struggle to establish shared values will be vulnerable to any storms (crises) of life that can potentially lead to an erosion of friendship or purity in a relationship.

Couples may appear to be managing well when an unexpected crisis such as a job loss, relocation or family conflict exposes areas of their relationship that are not supported by shared values. These types of events create stress on relationships. Couples that are not anchored by shared values can be quickly pulled in different directions. After a few years of neglecting their friendship, couples feel desperate enough to turn things around by meeting with a pastor or counselor.

## Enriching Friendship

One of the first questions I ask a couple in these circumstances is: "What do you enjoy doing as a couple?" Often this sets the tone for some self-discovery. They respond with things like ride bikes, hike, antiquing or sports. My second question pinpoints some of the problems, when I ask them: "When was the last time that you participated in some of these activities?" This question usually leads to some interesting looks being exchanged by them. Most couples I see usually respond with these kinds of statements:

- "It's been a few years since we were alone."
- "It's been a few summers since we took a hike."
- "My health has kept me from being as active as before."
- "Parenting responsibilities limit our time together."
- "It's been years since we traveled."

Couples need to identify the activities that promote friendship between them. Make a list of activities that promote friendship.

| Activities that we enjoy doing together currently | Suggested new activities that represent our stage of life, interests, physical limitations and availability |
|---|---|
| 1. | 1. |
| 2. | 2. |
| 3. | 3. |
| 4. | 4. |

Couples need to agree to try one or two of the activities on the new activity list. Not every item on the list will create a connection that enriches their friendship. Couples must not allow a few failed attempts at renewing their friendship to discourage them from trying to connect in new ways.

My wife enjoys strolling through antique shops. I can handle about two hours of looking at vintage furniture, jewelry, clothing or tools. As long as we agree that the antique shopping will not exceed two hours, we each get some enjoyment out of the experience. The time we spend together is an investment in our relationship.

## Other Characteristics of Friendship

*Respect*

I use the phrase "returned honor" to describe respect. Respect is best defined as an expression of love such as acts of service or random acts of kindness.

As a personal example, my wife models respect in creative ways. My favorite cold beverage was not available where we live for a number of years. In order to bless me, she occasionally drives to a neighboring state and purchases a case of my favorite iced tea. My favorite beverage shows up in our refrigerator a half-dozen times each year. Whenever I open the refrigerator door and see a green tea, I am always amazed by her thoughtfulness. My next thought has become: "How can I return the honor to her for blessing me?"

Showing respect to your spouse through acts of service is not about scoring points with them so that you receive the same treatment in return. An act of service or kindness is not about a tit-for-tat attitude or a bargaining technique that sounds like: "I will do this for you, if you do that for me." This type of "returned honor" keeps their relationship vibrant through regular expressions of appreciation or kindness without any expectation of payback. Couples can express respect through:

1. Speaking a kind word
2. An act of service
3. Purchasing a favorite drink or snack
4. Commitment to practice active listening
5. Being on time for events
6. Agreeing to participating in an activity that you would not do unless it was important to the other person.

## Dreams and Goals

Relationships have great influence over someone's future. Your relationships can be catalysts for a bright and hopeful future or they can be the tipping point of frustrations and regrets for years to come. Couples in healthy relationships encourage one another to pursue their dreams and goals, while unhealthy relationships can consume all your emotional and spiritual resources, leaving your dreams frustrated or unfulfilled.

The way couples support each other's dreams is very important. Supportive couples have the ability to help each other fly toward their future. But the reverse is just as true. An unsupportive husband or wife can sink his/her spouse's dreams. These dreams may include pursuing a college degree, participating in a short-term mission trip or starting a small business. A healthy friendship can be measured by the way couples encourage each other to pursue their dreams.

A common denominator among couples in a crisis marriage is the inequity in the amount of sacrifice that is extended to a spouse who is still trying to accomplish a personal goal or dream. Often, one spouse is required to postpone the pursuit of a dream in order to help the family become stable in the early stages of their marriage. Once the husband/wife has established a career, the other spouse may feel that their personal goals have been forgotten or are no longer valued by their spouse. Unfortunately, many men and women may never experience the encouragement or sacrifice required for their dreams to come true.

*In vibrant marriages, couples are committed to each other's dreams. But a personal dream should never be pursued at the expense of the shared values in your relationship.*

Premarital couples are responsible to choose a future spouse who is committed to their dreams and goals. Your spouse will have more influence on your dreams and goals than any other factor, including education, finances, friends or parents.

Your future is one of the most valuable resources on Earth. Each person's future holds all the possibilities of God's blessings and purposes for life and relationships. I believe that couples have unlimited potential to fulfill their God-given purposes (dreams and goals). Sadly, I have seen very talented and gifted people have their dreams frustrated by allowing selfish or self-centered boy/girlfriends or fiancés to remain in their lives.

Many talented and gifted people have been robbed of their dignity and self-respect by staying in dating or engaged relationships with people who are manipulative, angry, controlling, or bitter, because they thought marriage would somehow be the change agent that ended these destructive behaviors.

Unhealthy relationships require loving and devoted people to divert most of their energy and resources to manage abusive behavior rather than pursuing their dreams of vibrant marriage, family life, careers and service in the local church. These types of relationships literally suck the dreams right out of gifted and talented people. Couples must look more deeply than surface indicators, like attraction and compatibility, to determine whether boy/girlfriends or fiancés can be trusted with something as important as their God-given dreams and goals.

The following table helps couples identify God-given dreams and goals versus selfish desires and goals. Couples need to understand the differences between the two columns in this table in order to sustain healthy relationships.

| God-given dreams and goals | Culturally motivated dreams and goals become idols. These dreams elevate you above others. |
| --- | --- |
| • The gifts and talents that you have received from God are for the purpose of bettering the lives of those around you.<br><br>• Starting a business so that your employees and vendors experience God's love, grace, mercy and justice through your integrity and faith.<br><br>• Becoming a teacher so that you can extend hope and dignity and empower children and adults to discover their God-given talents.<br><br>• Completing an education allows you to gain influence in a specific area of the marketplace. Education allows you to bring kingdom principles into these areas of expertise. | • Other people's gifts and talents are used to make your life more enjoyable.<br><br>• Lying on a beach while other people serve you.<br><br>• Increasing your wealth at the expense of others' labor and talents.<br><br>• Hoarding wealth when others around you do not have the necessities of life.<br><br>• Homes, cars, boats or treasures become more important than serving in the kingdom and building relationships with people of different cultures, ethnicities or economic backgrounds from you.<br><br>• Your dream becomes more important or valued than your spouse's or children's dreams. |

Barbara and I have talked to hundreds of couples about dreams and goals. Many couples ask us: "What is the difference between

God-given dreams and selfish desires or fantasies?" We teach couples these principles:

- A godly desire (dream) allows you to serve others in ways that make their lives better. A person's spiritual gifts and God-given abilities allow others to find peace and purpose in their lives (Ephesians 2:8–10).
- A selfish desire (dream) places dreams and goals above relationships. Someone who is pursuing a selfish desire begins to isolate him/herself from relationships with and responsibilities to family and friends in order to accomplish their goals. Everything and everybody is a lower priority than the dream.
- A fantasy (dream) exalts the dreamer over others. The person pursuing a fantasy wants others to serve them. A fantasy becomes an idol at the expense of someone else's talents or dreams.

Christians are servant leaders who store up treasures in heaven (Matthew 6:20). Our main responsibility on Earth is to glorify God and demonstrate his love, mercy and justice to everyone, so that people will experience his grace, mercy and salvation.

*Couples need to evaluate their personal dreams and goals to ensure that they do not ask each other to make commitments to follow any self-centered dreams or fantasies.*

In no way am I suggesting that God is against accumulating wealth as a result of hard work, wise investments or faithful stewardship. God allows us to accumulate wealth in order to share it with others. Wealth becomes an idol when it is accumulated only for selfish gain at the expense of other people's prosperity.

The LIMRI worksheets allow couples to celebrate their strengths in areas such as dreams, goals and finances. The worksheets allow couples to discuss these strengths and to make plans to fulfill their dreams and financial goals (see Appendix D).

*Discussion Questions*

1.  Discuss your dreams and goals. Always show respect and support for each other's dreams and goals. Never criticize or be dismissive about each other's dreams or goals.
2.  How do you see your dream or goal as being inspired by God?
3.  Do you have any reservations about your boy/girlfriend's, fiancé's or spouse's dreams or goals?
4.  Are you confident that your boy/girlfriend, fiancé/fiancée or spouse values your dreams and goals as much as his/her own?
5.  Make a commitment to pray about each other's dreams and goals.

## Friendship Makes Dreams Come True

Barbara and I found ourselves at a crossroads early on in our relationship. From an early age, I had aspirations of becoming a pastor, so my marriage proposal to her went something like: "If you want to marry me, you need to know that I'm going to be a pastor." Barbara wasn't rattled by my declaration and she responded by accepting my proposal, so everything seemed to be settled. I had the dream to become a pastor and Barbara was willing to become my wife. But soon after my proposal, Barbara revealed her dream of wanting to become a high school basketball coach and physical education teacher. She wanted to attend a teacher's college in Dillon, Montana, while I wanted to attend a Bible college.

We soon recognized that an impasse had developed in our dreams and our conversation went like this. I said to her, "I guess we need to call off our wedding plans."

Barbara replied, "Wait a minute. I'd rather be married to you than go to college."

Unfortunately, our decision at that time in our lives reflected our immaturity as two teenagers trying to figure how life works. We did not have the benefit of pastoral counsel or mature couples speaking into our lives. Today, when we think about how we came to this decision, we cringe. However, God was faithful to extend his grace toward us in our ignorance.

When our big day finally arrived, and we became husband and wife, Barbara quickly caught the mother bug. She wanted to have a baby and start our family right away. This meant her focus changed from completing her education to raising two children. It was five years later, with two young children, when we made the decision for me to start attending a Bible college.

Now fast-forward ten years. I was serving as a youth pastor when Barbara came home one day with a big smile on her face, and said, "Grace High School has asked me to be an assistant coach for the girls' basketball team."

I remember the conversation well, because what I knew about coaching was that coaches are *never* home, especially on evenings and weekends. If it is not a game, it is a practice, and if it is not a practice, it is a tournament or fundraising. Do you see the hesitation I had about her coaching? I supported her, because Barbara now had an opportunity to live out her dream.

Eventually, the assistant coaching position led to a head coaching job with the volleyball team, which she coached for ten years. She was twice voted Coach of the Year. It was possible for both of us to fulfill our dreams. My dream was not at her expense, and her dream was not at my expense. We learned to make sacrifices for each other every day, because dreams require sacrifice.

For the last twenty years, Barbara and I have been teaching couples how to correctly pursue God's purposes for their lives. When a couple is equally committed to each other's dreams, no one has to give up their personal dreams in order to get married. The mutual support Barbara and I give to one another allows us to faithfully invest in our God-given calling to serve our community. Our jobs,

to this day, are an expressic
dream". The dream was to
of people as a pastor and a c
tionship was the foundation
dreams throughout our marria

> *As we look back on our lives*
> *that our dreams were fulfilled*
> *and our faithfulness to e*
> *that marriage made*

In the next chapter, we will look
ship (Stage II) to Committed Dati                    the Journey to
Oneness.

# CHAPTER FOUR

# Transitioning from Friendship to Committed Dating

**Friendship**  **Committed Dating**

**Second Transition**

The diagram above shows the transition from Friendship (Stage II) to Committed Dating (Stage III) of the Journey to Oneness. As discussed in the previous chapter, the Friendship stage entails communication, respect and supporting each other's dreams. The three characteristics of validation, mediation and financial management describe the Committed Dating stage of the Journey to Oneness.

## Validation

This stage addresses the need for validation in the relationship. Validation means to accept and celebrate someone for who they are. Couples in the Committed Dating stage need to validate each other as unique creations of God, uniquely responsible to glorify God through their gifts and talents as ambassadors of grace and mercy in the world.

Dating couples often struggle with this stage because both people must have a common understanding and expression of commitment to their relationship. From a cultural perspective, many couples do not use the word "commitment" to describe their dating relationship. Instead, I have heard couples use phrases like we are "hanging out", "seeing each other", or "talking" to describe their relationship.

In my initial meeting with a couple, I ask them to describe how they met, how long they have been dating and what their commitment level is to one another. At this point, it gets pretty quiet in the room. The man and woman usually look at each other and then at me without saying a word.

I will ask the man: "Can she (pointing to his girlfriend) go out with a guy tonight, have a nice dinner, great conversation and kiss him goodnight?"

He will say: "No way! We are exclusive."

This phrase has become the preferred way to describe a committed relationship. The dictionary describes "exclusive" as having the power to exclude or being limited to possession by a single individual (Merriam-Webster, 2011).

*The term "exclusive" is not a relational word because it implies power and control. Characteristics such as power and control should not have any place in relationships. By comparison, the word "commitment" is a relational word that describes a personal choice to be involved with another person. Someone who is committed to a specific person is choosing to avoid opportunities to develop other romantic relationships.*

## Validating Each Other's Views and Opinions

The word "validation" is a term used to substantiate or confirm something as being authentic or unique (Merriam-Webster, 2011). Validation is especially relevant when traveling to another country. Travelers must have their passports validated (stamped) by a customs agent to gain legal entry into that country. This type of validation does not require visitors to speak the same language or have the same political viewpoints. Likewise, for dating or engaged couples, validating one another's opinions and values is similar to stamping each other's passport. The stamp signifies an agreement to honor the views and opinions of their partner, even though they may not agree with each other.

*Couples must willingly validate each other as unique creations of God who are made in his image and who represent his priesthood on Earth. The man and woman belong to God exclusively, and their citizenship is established in heaven. Couples do not have control or power over each other. However, they do have a responsibility to respect, encourage and esteem one another.*

## Validation or Invalidation

The words that are spoken under duress will reveal the condition of one's heart. A heart that is prideful will be unreceptive to another person's attempts to engage in difficult conversations or disagreements. Pride creates dissonance between people. Humility creates space for differences. Couples who learn to express and receive words of friendship will successfully navigate difficult conversations and circumstances. The following questions reveal a humble heart:

## Discussion Questions

1. What do you want to be different about our communication, finances or leisure time?
2. How can I make it better for you? Give me one or two examples.

These questions can change the trajectory of a conversation and cultivate a humble spirit as couples discuss conflicts or difficult circumstances. Couples who desire to make things better for each other will promote closeness or bonds of trust that will sustain them through the most difficult times in their relationship. The Scriptures give a clear guideline that promotes validation. The wisdom from heaven is pure, peace-loving, gentle, impartial, submissive, merciful, mature and without hypocrisy (James 3:17). These characteristics are wonderful expressions of validation.

## Other Characteristics of Committed Dating

### Mediation

Mediation is defined as compromise or intervention (Merriam-Webster, 2011). I believe that mediation also means empowerment in relationships. Couples must learn to agree on how much time to invest in their dating relationships. Boy/girlfriends who demand that all of their partner's nonwork or personal time be committed to the relationship actually border on controlling or manipulative behaviors. Couples have many responsibilities outside of their dating relationship, such as work, friendships, hobbies, family and involvement in their local church.

*Healthy couples encourage their boy/girlfriend, fiancé or spouse to participate in these types of relationships and activities.*

One of the ways that couples can successfully mediate their time together and apart is to ensure that they are fully engaged with each other during dates or conversations. Couples who are texting, responding to email or answering the phone will communicate that other commitments are more of a priority than the relationship.

*Financial Management*

Financial management is the third characteristic of the Committed Dating stage. Many dating or engaged couples withhold information about their debt load from each other because financial mismanagement makes them appear irresponsible. Single adults need to develop a financial plan before entering a committed relationship, even if their debt seems overwhelming. I do not encourage couples to disclose their personal finances until the relationship enters the Committed Dating stage.

I have talked with a number of single adults who feel as if they are "unmarriageable" because of their debt load. Some people have chosen future spouses based on the other person's willingness to absorb his/her debt. Relationships that are formed around financial arrangements will have many hurdles to overcome in forming a shared identity. The person who has accumulated more debt will often be left out of financial decisions after they are married. A person's debt is not a primary reason of relationship failures. However, conflict over hidden debt or financial mismanagement becomes emotionally charged very quickly.

> *Each person is responsible to invest the proper amount of time to develop a spending, saving, and debt-reduction plan that demonstrates their commitment to make any present or future financial decisions on biblical principles and proven financial strategies.*

## Indicators of a Healthy or Unhealthy Relationship

Early in the Committed Dating stage, couples need to identify their strengths and areas of growth in their relationship. The healthy indicators in Appendix E will allow couples to celebrate what is good and the best about their relationship. Couples who identify any of the unhealthy indicators as being present in their relationship will need to make adjustments by creating boundaries to ensure that these behaviors change. Each person must be willing to change any of the unhealthy patterns of behavior that his or her partner has expressed concern over.

A couple that wants to avoid unhealthy patterns of behavior needs to take a team approach to their relationship. Healthy behaviors are learned behaviors, while unhealthy behaviors are a result of pride, arrogance or ignorance. If one of these unhealthy behaviors occurs in a relationship, the person who has been offended needs to communicate clearly to their boy/girlfriend, fiancé/fiancée or spouse that this is an unacceptable behavior. The person who is self-reporting or has been identified as engaging in unhealthy behaviors needs to repent, seek forgiveness and meet with a counselor as needed. Teammates hold each other accountable for behaviors that do not promote mutuality and respect or fall short of giving his/her best effort to the team.

## Teamwork

Relationships require couples to work as teammates. Teammates need to spend time together in order to understand each other's habits, preferences, and temperaments.

Receivers and quarterbacks must repeat pass routes hundreds of times in order to develop pinpoint timing. A 400-meter relay team must practice dozens of hand-off drills to know at what positions their teammates prefer to receive the baton. Likewise, premarital and married couples need to practice and show proficiency at modeling the characteristics of responsibility, emotional honesty, a shared spiritual life, communication, dreams, and respect in order to strengthen any underdeveloped areas in their relationship. Teamwork leads to teammates bonding over shared goals and dreams of success.

## Chemistry and Synergy

Great relationships have the "It" factor. The "It" factor is chemistry and synergy. These characteristics cannot be ignored in dating, engaged or married relationships. Chemistry and synergy draw a couple together and set them apart from other relationships. Couples lacking chemistry and synergy desperately want it.

Some people will define the "It" factor as attraction, but I do not agree. Attraction is powerful, but not sustainable. Just think about all of the celebrities that have looks and money, but who cannot find happiness or commitment in their relationships. I believe that chemistry and synergy are learned traits that are developed over time. Factors that contribute to this are:

- Connecting with healthy couples, such as parents, relatives, friends or mentor couples over extended periods of time.
- A history of developing and maintaining healthy friendships or dating relationships.
- Shared faith and values.
- Commitment to reconciliation through confession, repentance and forgiveness.

Humility is a key element of chemistry and synergy. Pride pulls the most attractive, wealthy, intelligent, gifted and spiritually committed couples apart.

## Confession, Repentance and Forgiveness

These relational disciplines allow couples to restore broken or bruised trust. Christian couples who withhold these disciplines from each other will be no different from a married couple that is held to the standards of a civil contract. These biblical values set Christian relationships apart from all other forms of marriage. Couples must learn to confess and repent whenever they offend each other, and then take the next step to seek forgiveness, in humility, without demands or entitlement. This third step includes extending forgiveness as quickly as possible, even at a personal cost to the person who was offended by self-centered or sinful behaviors.

Relationships will teach us that we are wrong more than right. I say this because we struggle with entitlement, pride and fear. The acts of confession, repentance and forgiveness are catalysts for restoring and enriching relationships. God never wavers in his resolve to love us. Unfortunately, our human nature is incapable of this type of unconditional and unwavering love. God is faithful to affirm his love for us whenever we pause long enough to confess, repent, and seek forgiveness after acting out in anger, fear, bitterness or pride, etc.

Couples should not try to transition from the Committed Dating to Engagement stage until they have demonstrated their commitment to confess, repent, seek forgiveness and extend forgiveness toward one another.

# CHAPTER FIVE

# Transitioning from Committed Dating to Engagement

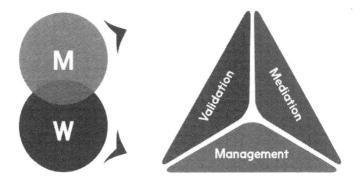

Stage III: Committed Dating

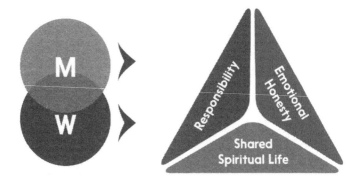

Stage IV: Engagement

The diagrams on page 58 show the transition from a Committed Dating relationship (Stage III) to Engagement (Stage IV). The level of commitment increases exponentially between Stage III and Stage IV, which is characterized by sacrificial love.

## Engagement

An engagement is a betrothal, defined as a mutual promise or contractual agreement to marry (Merriam-Webster, 2011). A betrothal includes verbal and symbolic expressions such as: "Will you marry me?" and: "Yes, I will", with symbols such as an engagement ring to make the agreement more formal and public.

Following an engagement, a couple must choose against forming intimate relationships with the opposite sex and disclose any friendships to their future spouse.

*The Sacrificial Love or Engagement stage means loving someone more than your own life. Men and women must be sure that their fiancé is mature enough to love them in this way.*

The only example of sacrificial love that I have found to be a sufficient litmus test is someone's personal relationship with Jesus. Love comes in many forms and expressions. However, no other love can compare to that of Christ Jesus, who took the judgment of sin on his body, ultimately dying on a cross in order to cancel the penalty of sin and death for all humankind. As recipients of this type of love, couples aspire to love each other sacrificially.

### When Should You Become Engaged?

An engagement should come after establishing a history of validation, respect and mutuality. I suggest that couples spend at least two to six months in the Committed Dating stage before becoming engaged. Rushing into an engagement is like going to Las Vegas and betting all your savings on "Red 23" of the roulette wheel. You can walk away a big winner, but the odds are stacked in favor of the house taking all your money.

Couples must then be committed to embracing the characteristics of responsibility, emotional honesty and a shared spiritual life before they choose a wedding day.

### Traditional vs Contemporary Mind-sets about Engagement

Traditionally, men are responsible to transition dating relationships into engagements. He does this by asking the woman to marry him or "popping" the question. This tradition puts men in a double bind. If he asks too quickly, he may be viewed as controlling or desperate. If he waits too long, he may be viewed as struggling with commitment. As stated earlier, each person may be at different levels of commitment in the relationship.

> *While it may be very romantic to anticipate being asked to get married, it should not be an exclusively male decision. Women have just as much to offer as men do in relationships.*

Women bring spiritual gifts, talents, careers and godly attributes into their relationships. In a contemporary mind-set, a woman is not simply waiting around for a man to pop the question. She is busy with her career, education, family, friendships and serving in the local church. The Journey to Oneness helps a couple to measure progress and maturity in their relationship in order to progress into the next level of commitment. Men will no longer have to make their best guess when the time is right to propose.

## Characteristics of Sacrificial Love

### Responsibility

Responsibility means that couples are committed to make life less chaotic and more orderly for one another. Another way to describe responsibility is to do what you say you will do. Responsibility includes commitments to faith, financial stewardship and personal integrity and purity.

## A Shared Spiritual Life

A shared spiritual life includes the practice of spiritual disciplines such as prayer, Bible reading and serving in the local church. Couples should be diligent about expanding their practice of spiritual disciplines. A shared spiritual life includes prayerfully seeking godly wisdom on behalf of your fiancé.

Couples need to be willing to discuss their spiritual experiences with each other by disclosing spiritual challenges, petitions, supplications and answered prayers. Your fiancé needs to understand how to support, celebrate and encourage these areas of spiritual formation in your life.

*A shared spiritual life does not mean that you have to enjoy or share the intensity or frequency of each other's preferred spiritual disciplines. However, couples must always respect each other's preferences and practices of connecting with God.*

One person may connect with God while spending time outdoors. The other may connect with God through the discipline of silence and simplicity. Couples need to share the insights that are gained from their devotional, prayer and worship experiences. This disclosure allows couples to know how to pray and develop spiritual conversations with each other.

## Emotional Honesty

An emotionally honest couple will validate the emotions and feelings of their fiancé, especially when one person becomes offended.

*Emotional honesty is showing respect and validating your fiancé's opinions or preferences, even when they are different from your own.*

Conflict or offenses that remain hidden or unresolved until after the wedding can result in trust wounds that can take years to resolve. These hidden offenses or conflicts will result in conversations such as: "Why didn't you bring this issue up before we got married?" A typical response is: "I was afraid that you would be angry at me for feeling this way," or: "I thought things would change after we were married." Couples must embrace this principle: "You can talk about a problem that you are having with me without it becoming a problem between us."

Premarital couples will learn to develop emotional honesty more quickly as they spend time with marriage coaches who can help them practice these types of skills as they review their LIMRI worksheets.

### Avoiding the Push or Pull of an Ill-timed Engagement

Another way to assess your readiness to become engaged is to identify each person's level of commitment to the relationship. For many couples, their emotional and physical intimacy is better defined than the level of their commitment to one another.

*People can be emotionally and physically intimate with someone without being fully committed to them. For instance, dating couples will talk about their future life together, and even discuss names of future children without becoming formally engaged.*

An understated or underdeveloped level of commitment usually leads to unmet expectations between the man and woman. When a relationship remains undefined, it can leave a couple feeling as if their boy/girlfriend has taken advantage of them. Problems arise when a couple misinterprets each other's readiness to become engaged.

A committed relationship that remains undefined for an extended period of time can stall out due to one person withholding intimacy, while the other is pressing for more. The man may feel that all is well, while the woman feels as if the relationship is at a standstill, or vice versa. In this situation, one person pushes for more intimacy, while the other pulls back emotionally and spiritually because the relationship remains undefined. For one person, the commitment level has moved into the Engagement stage, but their boy/girlfriend is comfortable in the Friendship stage.

*Many couples will successfully navigate between these stages. However, some relationships will not make it, simply because they do not have a language such as the Journey to Oneness to help them prioritize and express their level of commitment to one another.*

The majority of couples will eventually work through this awkward stage, but not without pain and disappointment.

My observation over the last decade is that young adults seem to struggle more with this transition than their predecessors did. Young adults do not feel prepared to develop committed relationships until their late twenties (Infoplease, 2015) and commonly say: "I am too self-centered to consider marriage at this time in my life." The longer they stay single, the more difficult it becomes to develop a shared identity with someone else. I know, from speaking with hundreds of young adults, that the vast majority of them deeply desire to form a shared identity with a future spouse but they struggle to build a bridge between the Committed Dating and Engagement stages.

## What Makes Relationships Go?

Relationships, like cars, need fuel. While gasoline powers automobiles, love fuels relationships. Love is a by-product of many components, like respect, emotional honesty, trust, responsibility, deference, faith, communication and conflict resolution.

### Emotional Tanks

An emotional tank is a common metaphor used to describe our capacity to love. These tanks cannot be measured scientifically, but understanding them adds great value to relationships. Most couples initially experience loving feelings toward one another, but in long-term relationships, there is a recognition that commitment, sacrifice and deference spell l-o-v-e. A relationship's emotional tank and a car's gas tank function in similar ways. Gas tanks ensure that drivers and passengers can get from point A to point B when they travel by car. Similarly, emotional tanks sustain relationships during conflict, misunderstanding, and crisis.

### Relationship Stoppers – Filter Failures

Gas tanks become contaminated by water and sediments due to filter failures. This results in poor engine performance and gas mileage.

> *Emotional tanks are susceptible to contamination whenever couples allow bitterness, contempt or unforgiveness to gain a foothold in their relationships.*

The only way that couples can avoid these negative attitudes from taking root in their relationship is to confess, repent, and forgive each other. These spiritual disciplines function like fuel filters in relationships and allow couples to purge their emotional tanks of unhealthy contaminants, such as bitterness, anger or contempt.

Left unfiltered, these contaminants can lead to couples being easily offended with each other. The smallest disagreement can create a total shutdown of communication. Couples will never be able to resolve conflict until they filter out these impurities through confession, repentance and forgiveness. Here is how to start:

1. Make a list of your offenses with your partner/spouse.
2. Ask the Lord to heal your heart from these offenses.
3. Make a list of the offenses that your partner/spouse has expressed toward you.
4. Ask the Lord to give you the courage to confess, repent and ask for forgiveness for these offenses.

## Fuel Additives

High-performance engines need fuel with octane levels above 90% in order to perform at their maximum levels. Mechanics will use octane-boosting additives to raise engine performance to even higher levels. Relationships are no different. Additives such as affirmation, kindness, validation, respect, humility and active listening always enrich relationships and increase couple satisfaction.

## Why Conversations Fail

I am captivated with the roar of a high-performance engine that is being throttled above 8,000 rpm. The only comparison to something as glorious as this is a couple listening and speaking in concert with one another. Communication is the power source in relationships. Couples who excel in communication avoid backfires and stall-outs when their relationship needs the power to resolve conflict and misunderstanding.

Engines need precise amounts of air and fuel in order to run effectively. Active listening is like air, while truth and grace is the fuel. For example, the woman asks questions or makes statements, expecting the man to respond with some level of emotion, interest or passion about these subjects. However, his response is always short or abrupt. She interprets his answer to mean that he is unwilling to engage in conversation with her. The conversation stalls out. Just like an engine with an unbalanced fuel and air mixture, the conversation has nowhere to go.

The following interaction between Carol and Jake illustrates why conversations fail:

*Carol wants to experience interesting and fulfilling conversations with Jake. Her conversations were filled with open-ended statements that would make it easy for Jake to respond to her. When she said, "I was wondering if there is a hidden agenda behind the school board's decision to wait until spring to do standardized testing," he responded, "I don't think so. Who thinks like that?"*

*Jake expressed an opinion rather than engaging with her question. Carol interpreted his response as an expression of anger toward her. He didn't understand that she simply wanted to have a conversation with him about the timing of standardized testing. Instead, he could have said, "I haven't thought about it. What are your thoughts on the issue?"*

Carol's question was the spark that engaged the communication engine, but Jake's question did not serve as fuel to move their conversation forward. His response caused a communication backfire. Carol's expectation of a stimulating discussion was frustrated by Jake's response. As a result, she gave up on the conversation and began thumbing through her magazine with no further interaction.

## Relationship Misfires

Couples that neglect any of the six characteristics in the diagrams on page 58 will be prone to relationship misfires. These misfires are like an engine running on only four of six cylinders. An underperforming engine leads to poor gas mileage and frequent breakdowns, resulting in frustrated drivers. Likewise, underperforming couples will be forced into the slow lane of couple satisfaction and left wondering why other couples are experiencing so much more satisfaction and enjoyment in their relationships.

## Benefits of Emotional Honesty

The capacity for emotional honesty is at the root of Jake and Carol's communication misfire. An emotionally honest person is able to engage in conversation with others who think differently, disagree with their opinions or are more knowledgeable about the subjects that are being discussed.

**Emotional honesty allows couples to learn from each rather than stand in opposition to one another.**

Couples typically enjoy stimulating conversations, but some spouses are inclined to end conversations whenever their husband/wife disagrees with them. This pattern of withdrawal is common when spouse's refuse to validate each other's opinions. If couples do not change this pattern, most of their conversations are played out in terms of the winner and the loser.

For example, Jake is uncomfortable discussing politics or community-related issues. He becomes anxious during these conversations because he feels uninformed on these subjects. Jake covers his uneasiness associated with these topics by responding with closed statements. Closed statements are conversation stoppers. He shuts down the conversation instead of asking Carol for her opinions on these topics.

Many couples struggle with emotional honesty during the early years of their relationship. Too often, they avoid discussing difficult topics or conflicts in order to keep the peace. Emotionally honest relationships take time to develop. Couples need to communicate regularly that they will respect each other's opinions, especially when they think or feel differently about the things they are discussing. The characteristics of trust and respect will offset any concerns of being judged for expressing an opinion that is different.

## Conversation Builders

In the previous example, *active listening* would have extended Jake and Carol's conversation. Jake could have paraphrased Carol's statement: "I hear you saying that standardized testing should be done earlier in the year?" He doesn't need to have an opinion on the subject to keep the conversation going. All he needs to do is ask, "Do you think this is a good or bad practice?" Carol would have been free to give her opinion on the subject and their conversation might have been more fulfilling for both of them.

Active listening helps couples avoid misunderstandings about subjects that result in communication misfires. The following guidelines will help couples to improve their listening skills:

1. The person speaking is able to complete his/her thoughts without interruption.
2. The person who is listening paraphrases the speaker's statements: "What I hear you saying is ..." and: "Did I hear you correctly ..."
3. The person who started the conversation confirms: "You heard me correctly." If not, the speaker needs to clarify what he/she was trying to communicate.
4. Their partner is now free to respond.
5. Couples repeat this process with each other.

Active listening skills take time and practice before conversations benefit from these disciplines. Premarital couples must prioritize active listening, because they may only see each other two or three times per week. Married couples have more opportunities to talk. But life does not slow down, and they will soon discover that talk time is often pushed aside by other responsibilities. Couples need to agree to make active listening their preferred model of communication whenever they are discussing areas of disagreement or conflict.

*Discussion Questions*

1. Review the characteristics below and rate how they are working in your relationship from 1 – 10 (1 = lowest and 10 = highest). Only married couples should assess the last two triangles.

**Identity**

**Friendship**

**Committed Dating**

**Engagement**     **Marriage Only**     **Blessing**

### Characteristics of the Six Stages

2. Pick one of the lowest rated characteristics and make a commitment to grow in that area, such as responsibility or communication.

3. Identify and discuss any areas of faith where you feel disconnected from your dating partner, fiancé or spouse, such as prayer, tithing, church attendance or service. Make a plan to resolve these differences. If you cannot come to an agreement that works for both of you, commit to meet with a pastor, counselor or coach as a couple before progressing to the next stage of your relationship. For more information about marriage coaching, go to lifeinmotionresources.com.

4. Is your relationship struggling from either person being abused in the past? Identify areas of repeated struggles in your current relationship that you feel are associated with these past experiences of abuse. Pray over these struggles and ask your fiancé/fiancée or spouse to speak with a counselor.

# CHAPTER SIX

# Forming a Shared Identity before and after Marriage

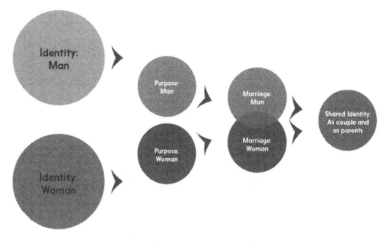

**Forming a Shared Identity**

The diagram above shows the progression of a shared identity that forms two "I's" into a "We" relationship. The personal identities of the man and woman transition into a shared spiritual identity as husband and wife.

We return, in this chapter, to Stage I, Spiritual Identity, to view it now from the perspective of a shared spiritual identity in marriage.

## Spiritual Identity

God created humankind to know him, experience his presence, and participate in the work of his kingdom. "I" represents the first letter in "I"dentity. Identity is formed out of our understanding of God.

*Jesus said to him, "I am the way, the truth, and the life. No one comes to the Father except through me." (John 14:6 NKJV)*

*"I am the vine, you are the branches. If a man [or woman] remains in me, and I in him, he [or she] will bear much fruit; apart from me, you can do nothing." (John 15:5 NKJV)*

These Scriptures teach us that Jesus is the source of our identity, and we are expressions of his righteousness, goodness and salvation to the world. A shared identity with Jesus means that we are joined with him. The "I" represents:

- The *way* of Jesus – his love for others, and power over sin and death (John 13:34–35; 2 Corinthians 10:4).
- The *truth* of Jesus includes everything he said about himself and accomplished, and his relationship with us (John 14:7).
- The *life* of Jesus guides men and women into another dimension known as the kingdom of God and the abundant life on earth (John 3:16; 10:10).

### IDENTITY Acronym

**I –** *Indenture –* You are not your own. You were bought with a price (1 Corinthians 6:20; 7:23).

**D –** *Dreams/goals –* Discover the God-given dreams and goals that he has put into your heart (Proverbs 22:6).

**E –** *Ego –* Your ego (will) is submitted to God's will. Your will be done … (Luke 11:2; 22:42).

**N –** *Nationality –* Your nationality has great value in the kingdom. Your nationality represents the fact that Jesus died for all. You are a testimony of God's grace to your people group (John 12:47; Revelation 7:9).

**T –** *Time* is a gift from God. God knows your beginning and end. It is all under his control. You now invest in the kingdom whether at work, home, church or neighborhood (Psalm 90:12).

**I –** *Interests* or hobbies are opportunities to share the love of Jesus with others who have similar passions (Colossians 3:23–24).

**T –** *Talents* – Your talents/gifting are expressions of God's character and handiwork in your life (Ephesians 2:8–10).

**Y –** *Your possessions* – Your car, home, bank account, retirement, etc. represent God's goodness to you. These things are under his rule. Christians store up treasure in heaven where moth and rust does not destroy (Matthew 6:31–34).

Our identity originates from God, our Creator and Father. However, secular culture denies these absolute truths about who we belong to and why we exist on Earth. Jeremiah 1:5 reveals that God knew us before we were born into the world. The world cannot add anything to our lives, but it can influence the way we think about ourselves (1 John 2:16).

No one can be totally unique from a human perspective. Everyone looks, sounds, walks, responds or reacts like one or more of the seven billion people on planet Earth. Any identity formed outside of your relationship with Jesus will be defined by your personality, relationship status, career, education, the car you drive, your financial portfolio or the clothes you wear. But all these false indicators of identity will fail you.

## What Is the Primary Purpose of Your Life?

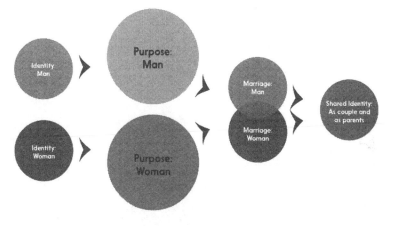

**Your Primary Purpose**

| | |
|---|---|
| The primary purpose of a woman prior to marriage is to glorify God in everything she does or says or accomplishes and to be an expression of sacrificial love, grace, mercy and justice to everyone (Micah 6:8). | The primary purpose of a man before marriage is to glorify God in everything he does or says or accomplishes and to be an expression of sacrificial love, grace, mercy and justice to everyone. Men and women share the same purpose (Colossian 3:23). |

Couples who validate each other's spiritual identity will avoid treating each other as personal property. In my opinion, the rising statistics of domestic abuse are due to spouses being treated more like property than like coequals and unique, unrepeatable, miracles of God. An abusive person needs to recognize that his/her girl/boyfriend, fiancé or spouse is God's son or daughter. I would not mess with God's child. He is our heavenly Father and, like a good parent who needs to protect and defend their child at all costs, God is able to defend his child and bring an abuser to justice, whether in this life or the one to come.

## How Does Your Identity and Purpose Change in Marriage?

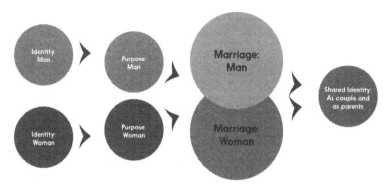

**Shared Identity and Purpose**

The diagram above shows the progression from an individual identity and purpose to a shared identity and purpose.

| The primary purpose of a *wife* is to glorify God in everything she does or says or accomplishes and to be an expression of sacrificial love, grace, mercy and justice to everyone, *especially to her husband.* | The primary purpose of the *husband* is to glorify God in everything he does or says or accomplishes and to be an expression of sacrificial love, grace, mercy and justice to everyone, *especially to his wife.* |
| --- | --- |

The identity and purpose of men and women remain the same following marriage. Couples are responsible to express sacrificial love, grace, mercy and justice to their spouse as well as everyone they encounter within their community, travels and circle of influence. Many of the issues that struggling couples are facing are triggered by prioritizing their responsibility of being a blessing to others around them such as neighbors, coworkers, or extended family and church members, rather than to spouses. Loving and serving others outside of your immediate family often leads to immediate gratification; blessing your spouse requires daily expressions of love and devotion that can go unnoticed. We love and bless others to honor Jesus not to receive recognition or compensation.

## Two "I's" Become a "We"

The average age at which single men and women marry is between twenty-seven and twenty-nine (Infoplease, 2015). Many of the women in this demographic have completed college, live independently, manage their finances, own businesses or work in corporate America, and serve in their local churches as volunteers and leaders. The same is true for many of the men. Currently, 60% of college degrees are earned by women (Perry, 2013) and they represent 47% of the workforce (U.S. Department of Labor, Women's Bureau, 2011). Single women also purchase homes in greater numbers than single men (Johnston, 2013).

Many Bible teachers interpret the Scriptures as saying that women must defer to men in matters of family, faith and church leadership. The statistics above show that women are well equipped to share in decision-making in all areas of life. Another cultural shift shows an increase of women enrolling in theological schools. According to the Association of Theological Schools, women make up approximately 37% of Protestant seminary students. Women outnumber men in completing master's degrees in counseling, and one-in-five Evangelical seminary students are women (Miller, 2013). They make up the majority of congregations and volunteer more frequently than men in their local churches. The Holy Spirit has equipped women to be expressions of sacrificial love, grace, mercy and justice to others long before they get married.

## Sacred Marriage vs Secular Marriage

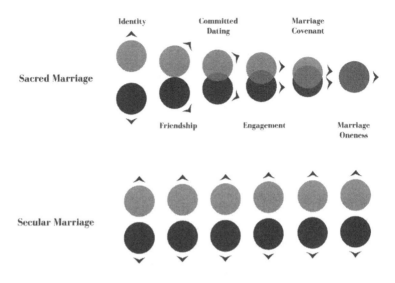

**Sacred Marriage vs Secular Marriage**

The diagram above shows the benefits of sacred over secular marriage. In sacred marriages, men and women are complete in their own spiritual identity. Husbands and wives form interdependent relationships as followers of Jesus and receive each other as gifts from God. These couples transition from "I" into "We" relationships. In order to sustain "We" relationships, couples need interdependence and serve each other as teammates in areas of family life, including budgeting, parenting, career development, leisure time and faith.

In contrast, secular marriage is like two "I's" saying: "You do your part and I'll do my part." The two identities involved in secular marriages do not have the benefit of being joined together in Christ Jesus. Christian marriage is based on two people ("I's") following the Lord while they are also committed to a local church.

In order to celebrate "We" relationships, couples want to avoid these kinds of assumptions of spiritual maturity:

- "God will talk to me personally, if he wants me to know something."
- "I know more about the Bible than my spouse, so I am best prepared to be the decision-maker."
- "I am the spiritual leader of our home, so do what I say."
- "I am not the leader of our home, so I am not responsible for spiritual or practical matters related to family life."

## Roadblocks to Forming a Shared Identity

Couples will quickly learn that each person's humanity tends toward self-centeredness. They will fail in many ways to create a sense of significance and security for each other, if they try to do this in their own strength. However, couples that anchor their significance and security in a personal relationship with Christ Jesus will be able to share in the blessing of a shared identity without the fear of being overpowered, manipulated or rejected.

## Identifying Behavior that Threatens a Shared Identity

In many cases, couples will begin to recognize the deficiencies in each other's character or talents within a few weeks of the wedding. Couples who validate each other as followers of Jesus who are responsible to fulfill their calling and purpose will be taking important steps to forming a shared identity. But couples will inadvertently threaten each other's need for significance and security as described below:

*Jake can make Carol feel inadequate when he points out her propensity to act before she thinks something through. He has often said, "You're like a loose cannon."*

*However, Carol threatens Jake's significance by making him feel that his cautious attitude toward change is an excuse that keeps him from pulling the trigger on decisions. She has often said, "Your fear of being wrong makes you indecisive."*

No one can always meet another person's need for significance, security or happiness. Marriage is an environment where couples must change behavior that threatens the significance and security of their spouse. Couples who ask these two questions will be able to create these environments for their spouse on a regular basis:

1. "What would you want to be different about the way I ..." i.e. spoke to you, approached household management and maintenance tasks, listened to what you are saying, or spend money.
2. "How can I make things better for you?"

### What Does It Mean for the Man to Be Head over the Wife?

Headship is used to denote a position of authority or supremacy. Jesus is the head of the church. His authority is recognized by all who acknowledge him as the Son of God. He trained up apostles and disciples to carry on his teachings concerning the kingdom of God.

The Bible teaches that the head of the church is Christ, and the head of woman is man. Whenever Christ is pictured as the head of the church, the body of believers is glorified (lifted up) due to the transformation that occurs through the indwelling of the Holy Spirit. The glory of God is manifested in the lives of his children as they preach, teach, administer mercy and justice, serve and become leaders in the local church.

Unfortunately, some people misunderstand a woman's unique gifting and calling as they read sections of the New Testament that depict men as being the head of women. Historically, the interpretation of headship was more about dominance over women. This is not a true understanding of the biblical model of leadership, demonstrated by being a servant-leader.

The dictionary does not recognize the phrase "servant-leader" because these words are opposites in nature. In our culture, a servant is not a leader, and a leader is not a servant, but the kingdom of God recognizes only this type of leadership. I am unaware of any culture that utilizes leadership in the context of servant leadership. This is what makes Christianity unique, and sets it apart from all other cultures or religions.

Nothing comes close to this unique expression of leadership in the context of men and women in secular societies or religions outside of Christianity. I want to bring my perspective to this concept of headship by looking at how God joins men and women together in holy matrimony.

In holy matrimony, men and women serve as God's hands, feet and heart to demonstrate sacrificial love to the world. The influence that husbands have with their wives should reflect these values. Men and women represent the body of Christ in marriage relationships. Jesus is the head of marriage and the church but, unfortunately, husbands often become a domineering figure rather than an empowering presence. The character of Christ should be consistent, no matter the relationship or environment – whether in the church or family life.

Why, then, has the wife's spiritual identity and primary calling somehow become secondary to her husband's? Christian husbands are responsible to stand with their wives to ensure that their liberties, as found within the New Testament, are fully realized. A woman's value is not determined by cultural or traditional viewpoints, but by her spiritual identity, which unites her with Christ to fulfill her heavenly purpose. Couples will benefit from the shared identity builders that are listed below.

- Consistent devotional life
- Sharing what God is saying or doing in your life with your spouse
- Attending worship services together
- Developing friendships with Christian couples
- Serving together

*Complementary Gifts between Husbands and Wives*

Jake and Carol are a good example of couples who benefit from each other's godly attributes.

> *Carol enjoys taking risks, while Jake prefers to calculate risk factors that could threaten their financial stability. She is a visionary who quickly sees the benefits associated with new opportunities. Jake uses cost-benefit analysis to assess the potential gains and subtract potential costs in order to limit losses. Carol has low fear while Jake is more fear-oriented.*
>
> *A "higher fear" index is not a negative attribute. Every choice, opportunity, event or decision should be examined to determine possible risk factors associated with new opportunities.*
>
> *Carol is confident that her abilities and instincts allow her to overcome obstacles that may keep her from being successful, while Jake intuitively assesses environments as having the ability to threaten their success. Together, they create a healthy check and balance in their personalities. Carol sees the possibilities, while Jake calculates potential risks.*

One of these attributes is not more valuable than another. Jake and Carol serve each other well as he lowers potential losses that could lead to financial stresses, while she courageously presses forward to overcome any obstacles to reaching a goal. Counting the cost is central to our faith. Jake and Carol become a faith-filled couple as they listen and defer to one another.

## How Does Marriage Enrich a Shared Identity and the Purpose of Family Life?

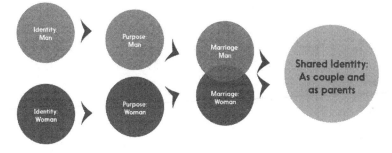

**Shared Identity**

> The primary purpose of *marriage* allows couples to glorify God in everything they do, speak or accomplish together and to be expressions of sacrificial love, grace, mercy and justice to everyone, *especially to each other and their children*. The spiritual identity and purpose that men and women bring into their marriage relationships are not reshaped, but enriched through holy matrimony.

Ephesians 5:21 serves as a guide for a shared identity: "Submit to one another out of reverence for Christ." The apostle Paul establishes *mutual submission* as the attitude that characterizes Christian community. He carries mutual submission into the context of married life (Ephesians 5:22–25). Husbands and wives submit to God, as do all members of the church. Mutual submission is a uniquely Christian value. Couples do not submit to each other out of a positional authority, but because each of them is a recipient of the same Holy Spirit, who speaks to the wife on behalf of the man, and vice versa.

The marriage covenant is characterized by submission, respect and love between husband and wife. Marriage can be described as a "horizon relationship". The horizon is the place where heaven and earth touch each other. The heavenly design of the marriage covenant exposes men and women to the godly characteristics of sacrificial love.

*Godly Submission vs Human Submission*

| Godly Submission | Human Submission |
|---|---|
| • Jesus is the Lord of all.<br>• Each person is responsible to acknowledge Jesus as their authority.<br>• Jesus is lifted up.<br>• The body of Christ is exalted.<br>• Husbands and wives are one in Christ.<br>• Each person is an essential part of the body. | • One person speaks on behalf of Jesus.<br>• A person is the highest source of authority.<br>• The leader is lifted up.<br>• The leader is exalted.<br>• Culture determines how men and women relate to one another.<br>• Culture determines the value of each person (abortion, genocide or caste system). |

Human submission is always played out in the relational dynamics of power and control rather than sacrificial love or servant leadership. Nations, tribes or governments assign value such as influence, education, position, royalty or gender to create class distinctions among their people. The kingdom of God is about each person serving the Lord, and using their influence, education, gender, authority and position to glorify him, and to advance his kingdom on Earth.

Ephesians 5:22 makes reference to wives submitting to their husbands. However, husbands do not define what submissive wives do or say. The wife is told to be submissive "as you do to the Lord". She fulfills her responsibility to be submissive by living out a Christ-centered life. As she submits her life to God, she models the characteristic of submission to her husband, and he receives a double benefit from her. He sees a living example of how to submit to the Lordship of Jesus as he watches his wife model submission in their home and in her personal relationship with Jesus. Husbands who feel responsible to instruct their spouses on what they should do as submissive wives and followers of Christ supplant what God has reserved for himself. For this reason, wives should not neglect their own spiritual development by defaulting to their husband's spirituality.

Husbands are instructed to love their wives as Christ loves his church. The same principle applies to wives. Wives do not define what love is or how it should be expressed to them. Husbands learn to fulfill the biblical command to love their wives by following a Christ-centered lifestyle. God empowers men to model sacrificial love to their wives.

Couples do not define the attitudes or behaviors of submission or love for each other. Each person is uniquely positioned to affirm behavior or attitudes that express sacrificial love, respect and mutual submission between them. Spouses need to listen to each other in order to develop sustainable and repeatable ways to model these attributes toward one another.

Many people will agree that women are more relational than men as they model loving behavior through multiple expressions that include words, self-sacrifice and acts of service in family relationships. However, the type of love that men express to God will enrich their wives' understanding and experience of sacrificial love. Couples double each other's understanding and expressions of godly love through forming a shared identity. Wives can fall into the same trap as men of supplanting what God has reserved for himself by self-defining what a loving and submissive spouse is required to do or say. Couples should not place themselves in the position of either head, master or slave to their spouse. The characteristics of love and submission are modeled best by serving one another as they do Christ Jesus.

The best way to encourage spouses to model loving behavior toward each other is to think about the ways that God loves and trusts them with the responsibility to advance the kingdom in the world and in their families. Couples need to help each other identify which expressions of love are most meaningful to them.

*Discussion Questions*

1. Make a list of the types of expressions of love that hit the mark for you and why.
2. Discuss these items with each other.

A shared identity is an expression of a Christ-centered lifestyle. Couples can only submit and love each other appropriately when God is at the center of their lives. At times, couples think that knowing the same things or having the same life experiences or understanding of the Bible will bring unity between them. However, these desires make couples irrelevant to each other, because neither of them could add new insights to the other's knowledge and experience in knowing and following Jesus. God designed men and women differently so that they would always have something to learn from each other.

Christians cannot place limits on each other's wisdom or spiritual discernment. This is not to say that whatever is spoken or interpreted as being from God should be acted on immediately. Each person receives godly wisdom and spiritual gifts which are unique to them. Couples are responsible to seek discernment together before acting on their spouse's words of wisdom or knowledge. Marriage allows couples to be recipients of each other's unique spiritual gifts and talents. In essence, couples double their capacity for wisdom and spiritual authority as they learn to share and receive all that is good from one another. The uniqueness rather than sameness of intellect, gifts, faith and talent allows two people to form a shared identity as a couple.

God joins the bride and groom to himself through holy matrimony on their wedding day. Couples can avoid relationship drift by being diligent to celebrate and build on their shared identity.

## Humility Is the Pathway to Spiritual Maturity

The Bible uses metaphors, such as sheep and children, to describe the people of God. Lambs and children are endearing terms that communicate God's affection for us. These metaphors communicate the need for humility and submission to Jesus. Sheep always need shepherds, and children always need fathers. We must never act independently from the chief Shepherd or the Father's words of instruction. Christians can build relationships with each other despite the many cultural, social, or economic differences between them. We all share the same Father, and each person is filled with the same Holy Spirit.

Believers are warned: "Not to think of himself more highly than he ought to think" (Romans 12:3 NKJV). People are not as spiritually mature as we may think. Spouses do not have intrinsic authority over each other because they have been saved longer or know more about the Bible. We do not climb a ladder of spiritual maturity that allows us to rule over others. We have been called to serve others (Matthew 23:11). Christianity is not merely based on what you know, but on who you know – Jesus, and your obedience to him.

## Spiritual Maturity

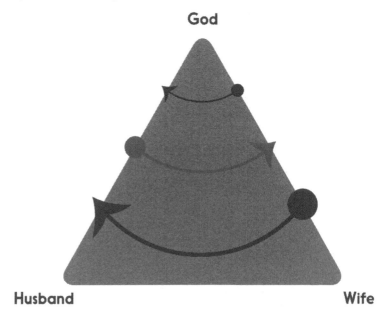

**Submitting One to Another**

The diagram above demonstrates how couples lift each other up as they become recipients of godly wisdom and practical advice from each other. The husband shares what he knows with his wife, and vice versa. Couples who practice both personal and shared devotional lives will always be in a position to share godly wisdom with each other. Spiritual discernment is not based on being saved for a longer period of time or knowing more about the Bible than your spouse. Godly wisdom is based on being submitted to God. This will always benefit the relationship.

A shared identity is not dependent on traditional roles or responsibilities between men and women, such as:

- Husbands work outside the home while wives stay home.
- Wives works outside the home while husbands stay home.

- Husband and wife both work and coparent their children.

A shared identity is based on being united to Jesus and validating each other's identity and purpose. Couples who celebrate each other's identity and purpose have a bright future ahead of them as they place each other's interests above their own.

I am often asked the question: "What if a husband and wife can't agree on a decision?" My answer is to seek counsel and find out what is blocking these two people, who love Jesus and each other, from agreeing with one another. In these circumstances, couples need to seek counsel and pray regularly about their disagreements. God will not withhold his wisdom and blessings from couples who seek him together.

Couples who expect their boy/girlfriend, fiancé or spouse to fulfill certain roles based on gender or tradition, such as the husband being the spiritual head of the home and the wife simply submitting to his leadership, can miss the benefits of a shared identity.

A man who position himself to be the spiritual leader of his family will often fail to recognize the gift of leadership in his wife. The same can be true for wives. They may submit to their husbands at the expense of blessing their family through their gift of leadership. I believe that God speaks as fully to wives as to husbands.

## How Family of Origin Impacts Marital Roles

Marriages are unique and personal. Wedding ceremonies were expected to reach 2.208 million in 2015 (Jayson, 2013). Every person has a unique relationship with God. Marriage represents the personal relationship that couples have with Jesus and each other, but everyone's family of origin will impact their marriage both positively and negatively. The following story shows how Jake and Carol's families of origin created expectations that they struggled to meet.

*Jake grew up in a loving home. His parents appeared to have a harmonious marriage. He never heard them discuss divorce or express any marital unhappiness. His mother was a strong woman with strong convictions. His dad was a gentle man, who always upheld an attitude of honor and respect for his mom. His mother managed the household and parental discipline, and served as the spiritual director of their home.*

*Carol grew up in a single-parent family. Her parents divorced when she turned eleven years old. She had a good relationship with her father, and was especially close to her mother. Her mom, a self-employed paralegal, was able to adjust her schedule to take full advantage of the time she had with her daughter.*

*Jake and Carol didn't spend much time discussing how they would work out the roles and responsibilities in their marriage. Jake assumed that Carol wanted to take the lead in areas such as home management and planning family activities. Her natural bent toward organization was already well established in their relationship.*

*Jake deferred to Carol as she planned their wedding. He followed the same pattern as Carol organized and decorated their new home. After all, she had such enthusiasm and displayed great organizational skills. She also was helpful in keeping them connected to their local church as volunteers in the children's ministry.*

*Jake was equally passionate about his involvement in their church. However, Carol did all the planning and organizing of their personal, spiritual and social calendars.*

Couples commonly carry remnants of their family of origin into their own marriage and parenting responsibilities. Even though Jake and Carol grew up in different family types (traditional and single), their parents valued togetherness in parent-and-child relationships. Neither one of them was allowed to spend much time away from their parents.

*Flexibility*

A spouse who grew up in a family system that valued togetherness may instinctively make decisions on behalf of their partner. The values of flexibility and independence can create feelings of disconnectedness for them, so most activities outside of work are done together.

Couples will notice that offenses build up quickly whenever one person is making all of these types of choices, even when things seem to work out well for both of them. In this scenario, the person doing all of the planning for social, spiritual and family events might assume that their spouse will enjoy all of these activities, all the time. They might also assume their spouse is fine with being left out of these types of decisions or choices. In the long run, this is not the best approach to managing these areas of their relationship.

Flexibility helps promote interdependence in relationships. Couples develop interdependence as they validate each other's strengths, personalities and talents. Interdependent couples take personal responsibility for home management, maintenance, personal and family schedules. Couples thrive in relationships that value interdependence.

## Mirror of the Soul

The Scriptures reveal the story of Adam and Eve. They took one look at each other and understood that they were uniquely different from all other created beings. There was an immediate closeness between them. Adam's first words, as he described Eve, were:

*"This is bone of my bone, and flesh of my flesh." (Genesis 2:23 NKJV)*

A fulfilling relationship is more than physical attraction, even though there was an immediate attraction between Adam and Eve. As a couple, they had a responsibility to care for and manage the garden. Couples need to move beyond their initial attraction and develop a "soul connection". A soul connection occurs when couples validate each other's identity, emotions, opinions and dreams.

Adam and Eve served as a mirror of the soul for each other. Adam saw the reflection of his manhood as Eve extended acceptance, love and deference toward him. He understood more about himself from one glance into her eyes than through all his interactions with the other created beings in the garden. Adam understood the physical and emotional differences between him and the animals. He was superior to them in every way, yet his identity was underdeveloped until he became a recipient of the godly attributes within Eve.

The same was true for Eve. Her identity was enriched as she became a recipient of the godly attributes within Adam. One glance into his eyes and she experienced love, acceptance and deference from him.

Even though Adam and Eve had fellowship with God, their identities were underdeveloped. God was a father to them, but he could not be like them. The father-and-child relationship formed a sense of significance and security in their lives. Adam and Eve gained a sense of purpose as they were given the responsibility to tend the garden and exercise authority over the animals. But Adam and Eve were limited to space, time and form. God, being unlimited in these realms, could not serve as a mirror of the soul for them. The marriage covenant is the catalyst of change that begins the formation of a shared identity. The characteristic of interdependence gives the couple a deeper experience of oneness.

John Macmurray, an Scottish theologian, said: "I relate therefore I am." God is the "other" person that we relate to who allows us to discover our true identity. Our identity is formed as he reveals his presence in our lives. His presence births a consciousness of identity in all humankind through his unconditional love for us.

*The same is true for a married couple. As they become the trusted "other" in the marriage relationship, they truly serve as a mirror of the soul for one another.*

## Discussion Questions

1. Discuss your conversion experience with your boy/girlfriend, fiancé or spouse.
2. What changed about your life after you became a Christian?

## Forming a Shared Identity

A shared identity allows couples to experience closeness in ways that words alone struggle to describe. The husband might be going through a difficult time but, as soon as he sees his wife, their shared identity lifts him above these negative circumstances. He no longer feels alone as he faces the things that are troubling him. The same is true for the wife. A consciousness of acceptance and love lifts her spirit as soon as her husband's eyes meet hers when he walks into the room. A consciousness of love and acceptance rises up within them as they look into each other's eyes.

> *Jake and Carol are learning to form a shared identity and to develop interdependence in their relationship. Whenever Carol walks into the room, Jake immediately feels better about himself. Likewise, Carol is filled with confidence as soon as their eyes met.*
>
> *Jake and Carol are quickly recognizing how their shared identity helps to create a sense of security and significance in their relationship, and that interdependence is better than independence.*

## A Struggle with Identity

> *Jake and Carol had been married for three years when they asked for a counseling appointment. Over the last year, they had been struggling in their relationship. A look back into their premarital file revealed a couple that was heading toward a vibrant marriage. They had successfully completed the premarital guidelines at their church that included:*

- *Knowing each other for a full year before their wedding day.*
- *An engagement of at least six months.*
- *Completing a six-week premarital class.*
- *Meet with marriage coaches for five sessions before their wedding day.*

*Carol and Jake felt confident going into their marriage after fulfilling all of these guidelines. However, Carol quickly became dissatisfied with their relationship. After talking with them, it was apparent that she was struggling to gain a sense of identity as a wife. Her career goals and married life seemed out of balance. She was hoping that her frustration and confusion in being a spouse would simply work itself out over time.*

*Over the last year, she had become more frustrated with her lack of self-confidence than with her relationship with Jake. She loved him, but felt as if she had lost her identity. She told him, "I don't know who I am anymore."*

*Her statement was both confusing and disturbing to Jake. He had always enjoyed her self-confidence and vibrant outlook on life.*

*Carol couldn't identify when she had begun to feel this way. However, she felt as if there was a blanket of indecision wrapped tightly around her. Carol had been very excited about the wedding. She was at her best when completing the many details surrounding their much anticipated wedding day. Planning and organization always seemed to come naturally to her.*

*When the wedding was over, her energy and excitement carried over into the details of decorating their new home. Jake had been more than happy to step back from the daily decisions of wedding planning and home decorating. He enjoyed watching her pour through the wedding books and home-decorating magazines. She was meticulous about everything she did and, quite frankly, she was much better at it than Jake. Carol could create a picture in her mind and then make it come to life. So why was she struggling with the questions: "Who am*

*I?" and: "How does marriage affect my identity?"*

A shared identity is unique to married couples because God has joined them in a lifelong covenant. Dating or engaged couples can break up at any time. However, engaged and married couples are responsible to encourage and validate God's plan and purpose in each other's lives. The identity builders in the left column of the table below will help couples avoid the identity busters.

| Identity Builders | Identity Busters |
| --- | --- |
| Affirming that each person is created in the image of God and is good. | Rarely speaking about the positive attributes in their dating partner, fiancé or spouse. |
| Affirming that God has a plan and purpose for each person's life. | Wanting your dating partner, fiancé or spouse to spend all their free time with you rather than serving others. |
| Encouraging each other to find a place to serve together in the church. | Refusing to serve in your church with your dating partner, fiancé or spouse. |

Jake and Carol were struggling with their transition from independence to interdependence. Most newly married couples need a year or two to successfully make this transition. In the first few years of marriage, couples will be challenged to make room for each other's strengths and personal preferences. Couples must learn to defer to each other in areas of home management, maintenance and decision-making, especially in areas where one of them is lacking in proficiency or experience.

*Discussion Questions*

1. In which areas do you or your spouse make decisions independently from each other?
2. In what ways can you share in these decisions?
3. What could Jake and Carol do to address this struggle in their identity?

**Heads and Tails**

Another way to embrace the mystery of forming a shared identity is described in this illustration of the quarter. One side of a quarter is called "heads", the other side "tails". A bank would be suspicious of any coin if one side were blank or disfigured. A coin serves as a fitting illustration of the "oneness" that is created through holy matrimony. God makes couples to be one, but not the same. Marriages, like quarters, have two images that represent two distinct personalities and genders. The "joining" of a man and woman in holy matrimony means to "glue [them] together" or "keep [them] close". Being joined represents the bond between a husband and a wife. Each person retains their personal identity, but now they share a new spiritual identity (see Chapter 8).

# CHAPTER SEVEN

# The Marriage Covenant

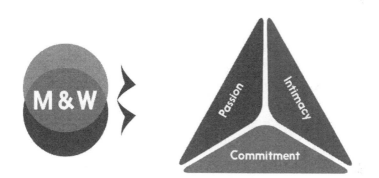

**Stage V: Marriage Covenant**

## Marriage Only

The diagram above shows the merging circles and arrows that represent the relationship between the bride and groom and their journey toward interdependence. The characteristics of commitment, intimacy and passion (physical intimacy) complete this stage of the marriage covenant. These characteristic are reserved for married couples, which differentiates this union from dating, engaged or cohabiting relationships.

## Commitment

The wedding day serves as the trailhead in a lifelong journey of faith, fidelity and family life. Commitment is a characteristic that empowers married couples to live in the direction of their pledges, promises and vows over the lifetime of their relationship, but it is not established by a one-time expression of devotion to each other. Couples must verbalize and demonstrate their commitment to each other on a regular basis. The bride and groom make commitments to:

1. Develop a shared identity in Christ (Chapter 6)
2. Friendship (Chapter 3)
3. Be respectful, trusting and trustworthy (Chapter 7)
4. Fidelity until they are parted by death (Appendix E)
5. Emotional support (Appendix E)
6. Physical intimacy (Chapter 14)
7. Financial responsibility (Chapter 4)

Commitment also means expressing the personal concerns and joys of your heart. Couples must be able to discuss what they are asking God to do in their lives and share any fears of the future that may be related to health, parenting, career or relationship struggles with each other, friends or extended family members. The statement: "I am committed to share what's in my heart with you" is an invitation to know and understand them spiritually and emotionally.

## Intimacy

Intimacy means to pursue closeness with your spouse in a purposeful and meaningful way, because it occurs at all levels of the relationship – spiritually, emotionally and physically. Couples who desire intimacy must want to know what is in each other's heart.

## Passion

Marriage invites couples to participate in the gift of sexual intimacy. Couples are now free to develop a sexual identity as they celebrate their newly formed covenant. Sexual intimacy is a celebration of the "oneness" that occurs through the marriage covenant, which includes your identity, friendship, validation and sacrificial love. Your sexual identity is celebrated every time you make love as a married couple.

Premarital couples who pursue purity and sexual abstinence will form a unique sexual identity. Abstinence is a spiritual discipline that serves as the foundation of purity. Couples who did not choose abstinence can recapture the holiness of sexual intimacy as they confess their sin against God and one another and practice purity and sexual abstinence until marriage. Confession and repentance do not fix past sins, but these steps can realign your hearts with God. He is able to make them clean and holy (1 John 1:9).

Sexual intimacy between husbands and wives does not have to fade over time. God's gift of sex is unlike our modern cultural beliefs that prioritize frequency, intensity and youth as characteristics of good sex. Let me say clearly that sexual fulfillment in a Christian marriage is not limited to any of these cultural beliefs. All gifts from God are lasting and can be renewed as we seek him. These God-given gifts are for serving your spouse and enriching your relationship.

*Sexual fulfillment increases with age because of the intimacy that is created through a shared spiritual identity, friendship, sacrificial love and covenant vows. Physical intimacy without these characteristics will lead to unrealistic expectations and false intimacy.*

## Marriage Covenants Are Better than Marriage Contracts

Covenants are based on an ancient practice that binds two people together in a business or interpersonal relationship. The Bible describes covenant agreements as unique relationships based upon mutual benefits for fulfilling your responsibilities and consequences for breaking your commitments. In biblical times, two people forming a covenant would choose an animal of high value, free of any blemishes. The animal was then slaughtered to symbolize their mutual commitment to honor God and fulfill their responsibilities to one another. Animal sacrifices also served as a warning to each person who broke the terms or conditions of the agreement. The offending person would suffer the same penalty as the animal for breaking the agreement. A marriage covenant means much more than these types of business arrangements. Couples repeat their vows, pledges and promises to each other and to God. In many ways, holy matrimony resembles the ancient tradition of covenant-making.

In today's culture, brides and grooms stand before God, family members and friends to pledge their love and devotion to one another until they are parted by death. The biblical understanding of covenant teaches that marriage vows are both bilateral and unilateral. A unilateral covenant represents promises that God makes to a person or nation. Bilateral covenants are mutual agreements between people (Jeon, 1999).

The bride and groom declare their vows of faithfulness and fidelity to God and each other during their wedding ceremony. Each person's pledges stand alone. This is the beauty of covenant. A bride and groom declare that her/his love is not dependent on their spouse's willingness to love them in return. However, a couple would never want to marry someone who was not committed to love them in the same manner.

### How Do Couples Fulfill the Requirements of Covenant?

Weddings reveal more than you think. Wedding guests are typically focused on the elegance, pageantry and intimacy that represent the bride and groom's love and devotion to one another. But in the midst of these amazing expressions of love, an even greater expression of grace is on display.

The redemptive work of Christ presents the bride and groom as holy and free of impurities or blemishes. As a couple declares their vows, pledges and promise of love and fidelity, God joins them together, ratifying the terms of covenant. But all married couples have limitations in fulfilling their pledges and vows. For example, the covenant requires couples to commit all of their strength, hearts and minds to the vows that are exchanged on their wedding day. Yet because they are human, at times couples will fail to be kind and compassionate and extend sacrificial love toward one another. Fortunately, God is faithful to love them unconditionally, even as they fail each other. God's unconditional love invites and empowers couples to experience and draw on a much deeper, divine love to share with each other.

*God is able to fulfill all of the conditions of the covenant, especially where spouses fall short of keeping their promises to each other. When couples fail to keep any of their covenant promises, they must confess, repent and seek forgiveness in order to restore trust that has been broken due to self-centeredness, pride or irresponsibility.*

## The Mystery: How Two Become One

Stage V is the destination that every Christian who has marriage in their heart dreams about – the miracle of the one-flesh union. This miracle stands in contrast to all other rituals or ceremonies used by other religious groups or governments to join men and women in matrimony. A Christian ceremony creates a miraculous event, whereby two individuals become one flesh. Miracles are unrepeatable by nature or science, making this a work of God – only God can join two people in this way.

Perhaps the greatest mystery in life is the joining of two people as one through holy matrimony. Wedding ceremonies have been witnessed for thousands of years, yet many attendees are unaware of what is truly happening to complete the "joining" of the husband and wife. Research shows that couples and parents are willing to pay up to $31,000 to participate in an event that is regularly misunderstood (The Knot, 2016). Most people understand the legal responsibilities of civil contracts that are ratified by the ceremony, but fewer grasp the commitments and benefits of a covenant marriage.

The very complexities and costs associated with wedding planning would suggest that couples want more than legal recognition and civil contracts to be at the core of their relationships. The Journey to Oneness will prepare couples to understand how two people become one, and why the marriage covenant is sacred and unique.

The English translation of the Greek New Testament word used to describe marriage is "one flesh". This means to keep close, to cling to or to glue together. These synonyms describe commitment levels that are unique to marriage relationships. In a Christian marriage, this joining is possible because both participants are filled with the Holy Spirit, who completes their union as husband and wife.

*Couples cannot be joined flesh to flesh. Contracts are used to connect people together, but holy matrimony is different. The Spirit in each person is joined together – Spirit connects to Spirit.*

The Scriptures require husbands to prioritize their marital relationships above all responsibilities to his family of origin. This principle is known as "leave and cleave" (Genesis 2:24 KJV). Even though this Scripture is directed to men, it is also applicable to women. In biblical times, the man stayed within his family of origin and his bride joined his family. In modern times, couples leave their families of origin and begin a new family of their own.

This biblical principle does not mean that couples love their families of origin any less, but their marriage relationship needs to be prioritized above other obligations. At different times throughout their marriage, spouses may need to be supportive whenever responsibilities to his/her family of origin take time away from each other. The Journey to Oneness will help a couple figure out when to prioritize their relationships over cultural or family obligations.

## Non-negotiable Standards

Couples who struggle with commitment and intimacy will discover that many unspoken, non-negotiable standards can detract from the process of becoming one flesh. For example:

- "I will never have a dog in the house."
- "I will always live near my parents."
- "I will always make the financial decisions in our relationship."

Some non-negotiable standards may remain unspoken for many years. The person with an unspoken non-negotiable such as "I will never have a dog in my home" may have experienced the loss of a dog as a child. Perhaps their dog was struck by a car when he/she was a child. Traumas like these can create fearful responses that appear irrational. In order to protect their heart from another loss, a non-negotiable standard is formed. Their spouse may be a dog lover who, as a child, was not allowed to have pets. A few months after their wedding, they have a conversation about getting a dog.

> *Maurice excitedly tells Patricia he was at the grocery store and saw a lady holding up a sign that said: "Free puppies for dog lovers."*
>
> *Immediately, Patricia replies, "I will never have a dog in our home."*
>
> *Maurice can hardly believe what she is saying. He responds, "But I'll be fully responsible for its care and cleanup. I've always wanted a dog, but my parents would never allow me to have one."*

Maurice is feeling controlled and is unaware of the unspoken non-negotiable or the deep hurt that Patricia carries, because she has never spoken about the loss of her pet before they were married. Patricia needs to reevaluate her non-negotiable standard because her life now includes Maurice.

More significant non-negotiables like alcohol/drug abuse, domestic abuse or financial abuse can also be triggered because of a couple's family of origin. Spouses need to have each other's best interest in mind.

These types of non-negotiable standards can potentially lead back into a pattern of independence rather than interdependence in the marriage relationship. If Maurice had responded, "If you won't agree to a dog, I won't agree to your desire to have a cat," it would have further hindered their ability to break away from and overcome non-negotiable attitudes. Couples who become interdependent will create a deeper level of intimacy and trust by avoiding these types of non-negotiable standards.

Intimacy is a doorway to the soul. Couples must learn to discuss statements like these in order to foster interdependence in their relationships:

- I feel secure when you ... call to let me know that you are running late.
- I feel validated or accepted when you ... listen to my point of view.
- I feel significant when you ... ask my opinion before making decisions.

## Discussion Questions

1. Are there any non-negotiable standards that place you and your spouse on the opposite sides of an issue?
2. Help your spouse to understand how these non-negotiable standards threaten your security or significance by finishing these sentences.
   a. I feel controlled when ...
   b. I feel insignificant when ...
   c. I feel detached from you when ...

## Love and Trust

A popular Beatles' song says: "All you need is love". Love is certainly a treasured gift in a dating, engaged or marriage relationship, but love must be defined beyond feelings or emotions. A couple must be able to match their emotions with actions and values of trustworthiness and emotional honesty in order to develop mature relationships.

The premarital couple who move toward a marriage commitment must learn to forge deeper levels of trust by successfully developing the patterns of trust in Stages II, III and IV of the Journey to Oneness. By doing this, they will be better prepared to make a lifetime commitment to one another.

Marriage is meant to last a lifetime. A couple will experience many unpredictable events and circumstances throughout their marriage that will challenge these trust patterns. Couples must be prepared to address the challenges that occur within each season of life. I have identified these seasons as:

- Newlywed: 0–3 years of marriage
- Home construction/children and parenting: 4–10 years of marriage
- Home remodeling: 11–19 years of marriage
- Heartland: 20+ years of marriage

Couples who value trust and trustworthiness in their relationship will successfully navigate all of the challenges that come with each season of married life.

A premarital couple can only *prepare* themselves for marriage. There is a wise saying: "You can't understand marriage until you are married." A couple can never fully understand how the marriage covenant changes their relationship until they stand before God, meet the requirements of the state in which they live, and commit to be with someone "until death do us part". Only then will they begin to understand the mystery of their one-flesh relationship.

### Trust that Lasts a Lifetime

The expression, "a trust that is given", has short-term and long-term advantages in relationships. Couples who have successfully developed trust patterns throughout the Friendship, Committed Dating and Engagement stages will see the benefits of these patterns and become recipients of this type of trust. Trust should never be taken lightly, and "a trust that is given" should be received as a precious gift. Trust is not something that can be exchanged in some type of bargain between two suspicious people. A couple builds trust by having each other's best interest in mind and establishing the shared values of purity, faith, fidelity and respect.

Trust that lasts a lifetime is a "trust that is *learned*". When a couple builds a history of trust throughout their marriage, they are equipped to address all potential challenges that could threaten their commitment to one another. The following scenario will illustrate how a "trust that is learned" allows couples to rebuild areas of broken trust in their relationship.

*Bill and Nancy have been married for seven years. Bill works in a corporate setting and Nancy works as a personal trainer. They came to an agreement that neither of them would spend time alone with coworkers or clients of the opposite sex outside of the normal work environment. Neither one of them felt weak in their commitment to the fidelity of their marriage, but they never wanted to leave an opening for a trust wound to develop between them.*

*Nancy had a casual acquaintance with most of the women in the department that Bill supervised. During a Christmas party, she became uncomfortable with a female coworker who seemed to need a lot of his attention. They discussed the issue and came to an agreement that Bill would be cautious whenever this coworker was around him.*

*Even though Bill and Nancy were confident in their resolve to honor their marriage vows, their coworkers and clients did not necessarily share the same values. From time to time, each of them had to draw appropriate boundaries with men and women who had approached them in ways that would have threatened the comfort level of their spouse.*

*They understood that men know men and women understand women. Their willingness to trust each other's judgment on matters of the opposite sex created an environment that protected and supported their marriage vows.*

*Bill received a call while at work from Judy, his coworker from the Christmas party. Her car had stalled on the way into the office and she was running late for a meeting with an important client. Bill agreed to pick her up so that she wouldn't miss her appointment. He didn't even think about the agreement that he had with Nancy until he was already en route to pick her up.*

*Bill became conflicted over his agreement with Nancy and the immediate need of a coworker. He called Nancy and explained the whole scenario right after he dropped Judy off at the office.*

*Nancy was surprised by his response to Judy's request. She understood that he responded to the need of a coworker that he supervised, but she was angry that he had not come up with a different solution to the problem.*

*Bill acknowledged how he had broken an area of trust and repented for his actions. Nancy extended forgiveness to him and they recommitted to honor their initial agreement.*

This story illustrates the principle of "a trust that is learned". Couples who fail to honor these types of boundaries will need to regain the ground that was lost through confession, repentance and forgiveness. Someone once said: "Life comes at you hard." Because this is true, there will be many circumstances that will push against the values that serve as the foundation of a couple's relationship. This is why couples need to agree on values like the one that Bill and Nancy established in their relationship, and recognize that all they value will be tested because life is unpredictable. A "trust that is learned" allows couples to reestablish any areas of trust that have been bruised or broken.

Bill must be willing to be trustworthy, and Nancy must be willing to extend trust toward him in order to experience a "trust that is learned". It would have been easy for them to fall into a pattern of a "trust that is earned" over situations like this.

### Discussion Questions

1. Where do you feel Bill acted improperly?
2. Where do you feel he acted properly?
3. How do you feel about Nancy's response?
4. What is good about a "trust that is learned"?
5. What concerns do you have with a "trust that is learned"?

### How to Reestablish Trust

Broken trust can have long-term consequences in relationships. An offended spouse is prone to place their husband or wife on "probation" for offenses unless they have established some history of trustworthiness. A relationship becomes threatened and emotions run high when boundaries have been breached. Trust wounds result when boundaries that are meant to protect their relationship are violated or ignored.

> *Every healthy relationship needs boundaries, and a vibrant marriage has established the value behind each boundary. The value of respectful communication forms a boundary that includes not screaming, calling each other hurtful names or interrupting the person who is speaking.*

A couple may also add a boundary like no talking longer than three minutes, and giving the other person an opportunity to respond to what is being said. In cases of extreme broken trust where there is infidelity, hidden debt, domestic abuse or any other serious transgression, a third person such as a trained counselor or a pastor will be invaluable to restoring trust and establishing healthy boundaries. These helpers can assist a couple to walk out honest disclosure through confession, repentance and forgiveness, as well as reestablishing boundaries that will enable the couple to rebuild a pattern of trust between them.

The value of "a trust that is earned" is contrary to the characteristics of "a trust that is learned". A "trust that is learned" requires the offended person to offer and extend trust to the offender, who in turn is responsible to reestablish the pattern of trustworthiness in their relationship. The characteristics of trust and trustworthiness are extended at a personal cost to each person. In some cases, the offending spouse will need to submit their schedules, spending habits, cell phone records, email accounts and/or purchase receipts to their husband/wife in order to validate that new patterns of trust and disclosure are being developed and walked out.

A couple that desires to grow and reestablish the trust pattern in their relationship will benefit from the TRUST acronym. This acronym stands for:

**T** – *Turn* away from activities that threaten the priority of family values.

**R** – *Responsibility* – Take the responsibility to make life less chaotic for your spouse, and do what you committed to do.

**U** – *Understand* that your actions are hurtful and become accountable for your behavior.

**S** – *Serve* together in a community of faith.

**T** – *Truthfulness* – Establish truthfulness by making a comitment to disclose any behavior that is inconsistent with the Scriptures and your family values.

The next step in restoring trust is for the couple to agree on a date, for example two to six month following an offense, to assess the progress that has been made in reestablishing trust and trustworthiness in their relationship so that they can celebrate the new patterns and behaviors between them. Without such an assessment, a trust pattern is sometimes only restored when the offended spouse chooses to pardon the offending person.

A spouse's "probationary period" can become more damaging to the relationship than the original offense. I have talked with many men and women who have been placed on a type of "probation" by their spouses for more than three years after an offense that could have been resolved much sooner with a little guidance from a counselor or pastor.

Couples who agree to honor the values of faith and family life will build up "trust reserves" in their marriage that allow them to reconcile any trust wounds that threaten their relationship.

## Discussion Questions

1. In what area (role/responsibility) do you desire help from your spouse?
2. In what area would you like your spouse to acknowledge or show appreciation that you are currently fulfilling your role/responsibility in your relationship?
3. What activities or attitudes do you feel threaten the priority of faith or family values in your home?
4. Where can you serve together as a couple? Serving together allows you to see the Spirit of God at work in your spouse.
5. Identify areas of self-protection that limit the emotional honesty between you and your spouse and commit to pray for each other.
6. List the values that guide your decisions concerning career and family life:

**Values of Family Life**

| Man | Woman |
|-----|-------|
| _____ | _____ |
| _____ | _____ |
| _____ | _____ |

**Career Goals**

| Man | Woman |
|-----|-------|
| _____ | _____ |
| _____ | _____ |
| _____ | _____ |

7. Identify any potential conflict between family values and career goals. Discuss ways to resolve these conflicts. Use the TRUST acronym to work through any of the differences that threaten each other's values or goals.

# CHAPTER EIGHT

# Marriage Oneness

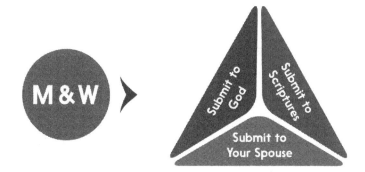

**Stage VI: Marriage Oneness**

The last stage in the Journey to Oneness captures the essence of holy matrimony. The diagram above shows the transformation of two individuals who become one flesh. The single arrow represents a couple's shared future. Married couples will spend the rest of their lives supporting and encouraging each other's dreams and goals.

## The Blessing

Blessing is the commitment that embodies the very heart of "oneness". The Marriage Oneness stage distinguishes marriage from dating or engaged relationships. The three characteristics of Stage VI are submission to God, the Scriptures and your spouse.

## Submission to God

A couple who submits to God as described in James 4:7 will ensure that their relationship is protected from arrogance and pride. These characteristics open the door for individualism and spiritual attacks and motivate couples to make decisions arbitrarily. These couples understand that the Holy Spirit is available to guide, counsel and empower their lives and choices. Couples are responsible to be wise stewards of the covenant that God has established between them.

## Submission to the Scriptures

Spouses who submit to the Scriptures will impart the blessing of godly wisdom to their relationship. The Scriptures serve as a compass for life and godliness and reveal God's commitment to his children (2 Peter 1:3). Couples who are committed to follow the Scriptures will discover a treasure of wisdom and strength that allows them to overcome adversity, trials and tribulation.

## Submission to Your Spouse

Spouses who submit to each other as described in Ephesians 5:21 will ensure that their relationship is characterized by humility, deference and validation. Humility is the characteristic that God blesses with heavenly resources and spiritual empowerment while pride is the characteristics that God opposes.

## Understanding God's Blessing and Discipline

**Heads and Tails**

The coin illustration that was discussed in Chapter 6 can also be helpful in explaining the principle of blessing or discipline. One side of the coin represents each person's love, fidelity and mutual submission to the other. The other side of the coin represents their commitment to submit their relationship and personal lives to God. These commitments will ensure that each person brings the blessings of obedience and fidelity into their relationship.

Sinful behaviors, such as infidelity, emotional affairs or hidden debt, etc., are rooted in one's disobedience to God and a willful transgression against their covenant commitments. Scripture makes it clear that God does not desire to punish his children for their disobedience, but his discipline is a reflection of his commitment to them as beloved sons and daughters. Godly discipline brings correction, healing and restoration to their lives. In my opinion, there is no way to experience a Christ-centered marriage unless couples live according to these principles of submission to God and one another.

A couple must therefore present all their plans, relationships and possessions before God on a regular basis. They must be willing to seek godly wisdom in order to avoid walking in their own preferences or strength.

I have counseled many couples who were unaware of the principles of discipline and blessing in a marriage relationship. A husband
may feel that he has a certain liberty to use unethical business practices without it affecting his family life. He knows that his actions are
contrary to the godly principles found in the Bible, but he chooses to
ignore the conviction of the Holy Spirit.

In a spiritual haze, men and women say things like: "I know God
is not pleased with me, but I'm not ready to change." The rebellious spouse will know exactly why things are going poorly, while the
innocent spouse is confused and anxious because of the chaos that
these sinful choices are creating in their relationship and family life.

The following illustration shows how far disobedience can progress in a relationship: A husband brings home a poisonous snake as
a pet. He decides against telling his wife about the potential dangers,
because he has always wanted to own this type of snake. His wife suffers a bite as he is trying to feed it. Instead of rushing her to hospital,
he acts as if everything is going to be fine. He finally lets her know
that the snake is poisonous. In his defense, he tells her that he has an
antidote, but his wife still suffers, because his self-centeredness puts
her at great risk. The antidote does not keep her from the dangers of
suffering a serious bite or living in a home that is unsafe.

Couples must love each other enough to put their spouse's needs,
safety and security above their own desires. They must be willing to
stop sinful behavior like viewing pornography, gambling, and drug,
alcohol or domestic abuse. Any hidden sin creates painful and traumatic experiences for an unsuspecting spouse. The sooner that sinful
behavior is brought out into the open, godly discipline and healing can begin to restore the offender and the unsuspecting spouse.
Spouses never have to fear the end result of God's discipline, because
it always leads to reconciliation and healing.

## Reconciliation

The three characteristics of Stage VI are foundational to reconciliation. Submission is the key factor in reconciliation for all relationships. I see dozens of couples every year experience reconciliation because they have understood what it takes to be humble, repentant, trustworthy, trusting and forgiving.

The fact that I can be very stubborn may stretch the imagination of a reader who does not know me. I affectionately describe these moments as having a "Ron day". On these days, I expect everything to go my way. I like quiet when I want quiet, and I like it loud when I want it loud. I like red lights to turn green just as I approach them, and I like it when people let me in and out of traffic whenever it is convenient for me.

When I am stuck in a "Ron day" or week, my desires always take priority over the needs of others. Not only are the needs of others a low priority, but also the plans and purposes of God are not on my "Top Ten List" to accomplish that day. My self-centeredness creates conflict between me and the people I am committed to love and serve. Whenever I place my personal desires above the needs of others, I am no longer trusting that God has my best interest in mind. My goal is to make things happen at my pace and priority. These self-centered attitudes and behaviors are contrary to humility and servanthood.

God's discipline redirects me toward the sacrificial love that I pledged to my wife and family, but it is never a form of *punishment.* God disciplines us in ways that are unique to our relationship with him. He does not use a discipline chart that matches a sin with a particular consequence. He works discipline into the daily activities of our lives, so that we will acknowledge our self-centered ways and repent of any behavior or attitude that is contrary to godly character. His discipline is an expression of his love for us.

God is very creative with his discipline in my life. He usually gets my attention when my day becomes full of delays and time management goes out the window. For me, these scenarios are contrary to what the blessing of God typically brings into my life. Usually, my relationships with coworkers and family members are harmonious, and proper time management allows me to work effectively. Whenever these blessings are withheld from me, my life does not work well. I am a little thickheaded, but it does not take long for me to come to the conclusion that my self-centered ways are the catalyst for the discipline that I am experiencing. With that awareness, I am able to come to God with repentance. He faithfully repositions me on the pathway that is best for my marriage, family and work.

Godly discipline plays out uniquely in marriage relationships. In my experience as a pastor of reconciliation, I have seen a principle at work that is rarely discussed. The godly discipline that redirects husbands also affects their wives, and vice versa. Whenever I am disobedient to God and his Word, his discipline has an effect on my wife. Barbara and I share a spiritual identity, and our self-centered or sinful behavior will bring the discipline of God into our relationship.

The same is true about blessings. Our obedience is rewarded with his presence, and is extended to our spouse. Couples must remember that godly discipline is not about punishment, but training in righteousness and peace with God (Hebrews 12:5–6, 10–11).

## Your Future Belongs to God Alone

Stage VI, Marriage Oneness, encourages couples to be risk takers as they consider their value and purpose in the kingdom of God. They are not together by chance but by his or her choice. Couples commonly believe that God has woven their futures together. The Bible teaches that God knows everything about us – our successes, failures, and even the number of hairs on our heads (Matthew 10:30). He knows who will remain single, marry, divorce or remarry. He also knows how many children we will or will not bring into the world.

Omniscience means that God is "all-knowing". He knows

everything before it happens. Our lives and relationships are enriched by seeking his "yes" or "no" to our choices, prayers and personal needs. A "no" from God is as good as a "yes" because, whatever his answer, we will receive his best for our lives.

From the beginning of time, God has bound our future directly to him. He created us to know and to experience his presence through our dreams, goals, hobbies, careers, ministries, relationships and family life. While he allows us to develop a shared identity with our spouse, our future is reserved for him. If our future were joined to another human being, our ability to experience joy, peace and happiness would be extremely limited.

*A follower of Jesus does not have to fear being unloved or rejected by God. He would never choose to love one of his children less nor value one over another.*

God is not like a baseball card enthusiast or collector. A collector judges the value of a card on the popularity or success of the player. God is not like this. He would never trade you for a more popular player. For instance, Mickey Mantle and Willie Mays were great baseball players. Both of these men will always be revered when people talk about their accomplishment. But because we live in a market-driven economy, most collectors would gladly exchange their Willie Mays for a Mickey Mantle card because one has more value than the other, even though each of their records and popularity will forever make them icons of baseball history.

*Someone's value or worth is not dependent on their accomplishments or how other people feel about them. God loves you just as you are and would never trade you for anyone else.*

We are God's children and he is committed to fulfill his purposes in our lives. God created us to share an identity with him throughout eternity.

## Your Future Is Secure in God

This stage helps couples to consider how their personal choices and preferences will impact their spouse and children. The story below shows how these personal choices can affect your spouse's future.

> *Jake decided to take up the sport of hang gliding. His skills developed to the point where he was able to take the jump of a lifetime. He ran toward the edge of the 4,000-foot plateau, made the leap and lifted majestically into the sky. Tragically, a downdraft pushed him into the side of the mountain and he fell to the ground. Carol became a widow as the result of Jake's passion for adventure. She was left alone to manage life and parent their children alone.*
>
> *What about Carol's future? Was it altered by Jake's decision to take up hang gliding?*

We would hope that our spouse would always have our best interest in mind – even when choosing hobbies, careers or physical activities. Unfortunately, that is not always the case. The push for adventure, success and prosperity has led many men and women to place their marriage in a secondary position to their own drive for accomplishments. Spouses commonly say: "I started this business, purchased this boat or took this job for the benefit of our family," when actually it was nothing more than a selfish desire on their part.

I have met wonderful Christian men and women who chose to commit adultery, begin emotional affairs, or become violent and controlling toward their spouses. Is this the type of future that God had destined for their spouses? I say, "No!"

***Your future can include suffering from the consequences of poor decisions, a poor economy, natural disasters or a crisis marriage, but the hope of a better future is not defined by these events.***

Robert Schuller may have said it best when he observed that: "Joy is not the absence of suffering, but the presence of God." Your future can be negatively influenced by your sinful bents or by self-centered actions of friends or family members, but your future is totally secure in the hands of a loving God. He will always be in our corner and his presence will always be with us, no matter how difficult or challenging things become.

# CHAPTER NINE

# The Change Process

## Defining Change

One of the key indicators of a vibrant relationship is an ability to embrace change. Merriam-Webster (2011) defines "change" as making the form, nature or content of something different from what it was originally. Heraclitus' wise statement is well known: "The only thing that is constant is change." This is actually good news for all relationships.

In the Journey to Oneness, the first pathway to change is motivated by your own need to grow and mature as a believer in Christ Jesus. The second pathway to change comes as *your fiancé or spouse* grows and matures as a believer in Christ Jesus. The Holy Spirit is the source of these transformations. He convicts of sin and empowers believers with an ability to reflect the humility of Jesus.

In the premarital relationship, God initiates changes in the man and woman in order to prepare them to share an identity as husband and wife. The man invites the woman to share in his identity as a son of God, and the woman invites the man to share in her identity as a daughter of God. In the marriage relationship, God sometimes uses the husband as a catalyst for change, and at other times he uses the wife as the initiator of change. The outcome of these changes always benefits the relationship. God is not about changing just one spouse in the marriage relationship, because he has joined them to be "as one" in Christ Jesus.

*Mutuality* is another way to think about changes within marriage relationships. Jack Balswick writes in his book, *The Family*: "Mutuality is a key principle behind a family covenant." It is important to realize that God also uses children to initiate change in their parents' lives. A marriage covenant sets a family apart from any other type of relationship. The changes initiated by the Holy Spirit are always good and for the best of all family members, unlike some change that is initiated by personal preferences or selfish motivations, which often leads to control and manipulation.

This understanding of mutuality and the Change Process can help couples and families to embrace the benefits of transforming relationships that allow family members to "get on the same side of change".

I believe that the greatest illustration of change is found in the Scriptures:

*"And we know that in all things God works for the good of those who love him, who have been called according to his purpose. For those God foreknew he also predestined to be conformed to the likeness of his Son, that he might be the firstborn among many brothers and sisters. And those he predestined, he also called; those he called, he also justified; those he justified, he also glorified." (Romans 8:28–30)*

The words *called*, *justified* and *glorified* highlight essential steps of spiritual growth and reveal how God engages us in this Change Process.

- To be *called* means that God has invited us to follow him. He initially calls each of us into a change process by bringing us out of the darkness and into the light. He uses events, circumstances and choices to develop godly character and spiritual maturity in us.

- To be *justified* is a legal term that places us in a position of innocence, even though we are guilty of rebellion toward God. Jesus' obedience to God and his substitutionary death on the cross mean that we are set free of the penalty of God's judgment.

- To be *glorified* means that God has empowered us to be ambassadors of his righteousness and holiness. His weight or character rests on us.

Unfortunately, a couple may resist opportunities for change because one partner feels he/she is being manipulated or controlled by their fiancé or spouse. I have heard many spouses say to each other: "I have changed enough for you." This statement is one of the most harmful responses that spouses can give each other.

*A spouse who says, "I have changed enough for you," has lost sight of the nature and purpose of change. We change in order to become more like Jesus. Change is not for the purpose of trying to please your spouse, so that you become more of what they want you to be.*

Both individuals are imperfect and in a process of change. Someone who is reluctant to embrace opportunities to change something about their character, behavior or temperament must ask why they resist or fear to do so.

In order to set an appropriate response to change, I ask couples to respond to the following question: "What types of things do you experience when you enter into God's presence?" People commonly say things like peace, love, wisdom or forgiveness. My second question is: "What do you need to exchange with God in order to benefit from receiving these divine attributes?"

Couples are often stumped by this question. Many people believe that all they have to do is simply to ask for godly wisdom and they will receive what they need. I believe that people must be willing to surrender their struggles with anger, fear, shame, anxiety or guilt to God in order to receive his peace, hope and courage for their lives.

| Exchanging your struggles | By receiving his divine attributes |
|---|---|
| I give you my bitterness or judgment toward … | I need your healing for my heart and your forgiveness in my relationships with … |
| I give you my anger toward … | I need your presence to rule over my emotions. |
| I give you my fear and anxiety about … | I need your hope and protection. |
| I give you my doubt. | I need your wisdom. |

Christians need to let go of their fear, anger, bitterness or worldly wisdom in order to receive what God has to offer them. Someone who is asking for God's forgiveness may need to exchange an attitude of unforgiveness that he/she may be harboring toward others by praying something like: "Father, I am struggling with bitterness and resentment toward my spouse. I am asking for more of your grace so that I can forgive them."

Someone who is seeking godly wisdom may need to relinquish their preferred way of doing things and trust in the Lord by praying: "Father, I want to buy a new home, but I want your blessing on this decision. I ask for your wisdom and guidance (Proverbs 3:5–6)."

These kinds of prayers can bring about spiritual maturity in husbands and wives.

## The Change Process

The hope of every Christian is to become more like Jesus. The Change Process will give couples unique ways to experience more of God's love, mercy and justice in their relationship.

**Unhappy or Dissatisfied**          **God**

Blame                                                Reconciliation

Blind/Deaf

Convince                                          Hope

Offended

Acceptance

Resist

Compounded

### The Change Process

Most people ask their spouse for change when they are unhappy or dissatisfied about something in their relationship. Couples will quickly learn that unhappiness and dissatisfaction are poor motivators for change. Typically, if one person is expressing dissatisfaction, the other person feels responsible for these feelings. Couples will quickly find themselves on opposite sides of the Change Process.

The right side of the scale in the illustration on page 124 represents the woman and the left side the man. Her unhappiness creates a downward movement on the right side of the scale, while his side moves upward. The husband feels responsible for creating an imbalance between them. This is a common reaction when spouses express unhappiness or dissatisfaction to each other.

**Relational Imbalance**

The left side of the Change Process in the diagram on page 123, Unhappy or Dissatisfied, comprises six stages:

1. Blame
2. Blind/Deaf
3. Convince
4. Offended
5. Resist
6. Compounded (offenses)

This process will not result in mutually beneficial changes between spouses. Most couples will find themselves on opposite sides of change whenever they engage their spouse too early in the Change Process.

God uses relationships as catalysts to develop faith and maturity in a relationship. Whenever spouses experience the conviction of the Holy Spirit, he/she needs to spend time in prayer in order to discern whether change is needed on a personal level or in their relationship. A person should only ask their spouse to enter a change process if they are unable to resolve these feelings after seeking godly wisdom.

The spouse who takes their unhappiness or dissatisfaction to their husband or wife before seeking godly wisdom through prayer may hear something like: "You need to change," rather than: "I believe that God wants to change something in the way we relate to one another." Most spouses would prefer to hear the second statement rather than the first.

*It is important to remember that God is most concerned about your willingness to become more like Jesus. He is the one who can change your spouse as needed.*

The Change Process allows you to focus on the growth plan that God has for your life. Trust God to draw your spouse into a deeper relationship with him.

### Blame Stage

The Blame stage is the first roadblock in the Change Process. Spouses who share their unhappiness or dissatisfaction with each other before taking it to God will put their husband/wife in an awkward position to resolve these negative feelings. The spouse will often feel as if she/he is being blamed for their husband or wife's unhappiness or negative feelings.

A conversation in the Blame Stage may sound like this: "I don't like the way you are treating me."

The spouse responds: "What are you talking about? I respect and love you."

The conversation will often spiral downward from this point, because one spouse feels blamed for an offense that they are unaware of committing.

### Blind/Deaf Stage

The Blind/Deaf stage is the second roadblock in the Change Process. In relationships, it is common for one person to have a higher level of marital satisfaction than their spouse. In many cases, both spouses are unaware of each other's struggle with unhappiness or dissatisfaction.

The person who is being confronted may not feel the same way or agree that what their spouse is describing are elements of dissatisfaction or unhappiness. The conversation may go something like this:

- "I don't have a look on my face; you are misreading my expressions."
- "I don't have a tone in my voice; you are hearing something that I am not trying to express to you."
- "I don't feel disconnected from you."

### Convince Stage

The Convince stage is the third roadblock in the Change Process. Couples will become stuck in this stage by not validating each other's requests for change or appear to be dismissive toward the relevance of their spouse's requests. At this point, couples will find themselves in the downward slope of the Change Process.

The downward slope (see the diagram on page 123) of the Convince stage begins when one person in the relationship says: "I am unhappy with the way you communicate with me."

The other person responds: "I don't know what you're talking about. How long have you felt this way?"

The person who is unhappy or dissatisfied begins to recount the events and circumstances that make them feel this way. Conversations may go something like this:

- "Last week when you ..."
- "Last month when you ..."
- "On our vacation last year, you did this or that ..."

Sometimes, an unhappy or dissatisfied person will bring up memories of unhappiness or dissatisfaction from many years ago, going back to the beginning of their marriage: "On our honeymoon night you didn't …"

The Convince stage can become overwhelming for the person who is feeling blamed for these negative emotions or memories.

### Offended Stage

The Offended stage is the fourth roadblock in the Change Process. The person who is unhappy or dissatisfied is now offended. They were hoping their spouse would be more sympathetic or motivated to participate in a change process. Unfortunately, the Blame, Blind and Convince stages are poor environments for nurturing change in relationships, where each person experiences the benefits of collaboration. At this point, one person feels as if they are being asked to do all of the changing or must agree that everything their spouse says is accurate.

### Resist Stage

The Resist stage is the fifth roadblock in the Change Process. The person who feels blamed usually responds to past events and details as an indictment against their character. Spouses may say something like:

- "You are not the easiest person to live with!"
- "I could bring up things that make me unhappy or dissatisfied, but I choose to keep things like that to myself."

The Resist stage is motivated by a need to protect yourself against criticism or blame.

### Compounded Offenses Stage

The Compounded Offenses stage is the sixth roadblock in the Change Process. The person who is feeling blamed is offended by hearing about all of these past events or circumstances that did not meet the expectations of their spouse. The relationship is now struggling with a compounded offense. Both spouses are offended by each other. One spouse is offended because they feel stonewalled, while the other person feels blamed.

The Compounded Offense stage can be avoided by taking any unhappiness or dissatisfaction to God before expressing it to your spouse. At times, relationships trigger areas in a person's life that they need to address before discussing these things with their spouse. Some of these issues include unrealistic expectations, entitlement and controlling attitudes. Some couples rarely move past the left side of the Change Process because they do not take their unhappiness to God or discuss their feelings and emotions with a friend, pastor or counselor before talking to their spouse.

The right side of the Change Process in the diagram on page 123, Turning to God, includes three stages:

1. Acceptance
2. Hope
3. Reconciliation

### Acceptance Stage

The Acceptance stage is the first step toward "couples getting on the same side of change". Couples who have taken their unhappiness or dissatisfaction to the Lord as an opportunity to grow in their personal faith and dependence on him will be highly respected by their spouse.

One of the most elementary principles of Christianity is change. The wise must become foolish, the rich must become humble, and the strong must become weak in order to become more like Jesus. Unfortunately, people resist change that does not put them in a position of power. Spouses who say: "I have changed enough for you," are missing an opportunity to bring the presence of Jesus into their relationship. Spouses are responsible to help each other to become more like Jesus. The outcome of change is to become more Christ-like.

> *Sometimes God initiates change as the man asks his wife to enter a change process with him. At other times, God initiates change as the woman asks the man to enter a change process with her. Change is the catalyst to become a mature follower of Christ Jesus.*

Couples who embrace the benefits of change will be able to express deeper levels of sacrificial love toward one another.

Change affects both people in a relationship. Couples begin the Change Process by accepting an opportunity to pray together to become more Christ-like. The following questions allow couples to move toward one another in a spirit of love and deference:

- "What do you want to be different about …?"
- "How can I make it better for you?"

## Hope Stage

The Hope stage begins when couples lay down their preferred outcomes of change and apply biblical wisdom to their relationship. Couples need to open up their hearts to the Scriptures in order to gain a godly perspective on the type of change that is being initiated by the Holy Spirit in their relationship.

> *Carol tells her husband, Jake, "I feel as if you are impatient with me. Your impatience makes me feel judged and incompetent."*
>
> *Jake doesn't try to deflect or resist Carol's statement. He asks, "Do I become impatient with you over certain events or circumstances?"*
>
> *Carol says, "When it comes to money, I feel that you are very impatient with me. I feel like you don't trust me to spend our money wisely."*

Jake and Carol take this request for change to the Lord and read the following Scripture:

*But the fruit of the Spirit is love, joy, peace, forbearance, kindness, goodness, faithfulness, gentleness and self-control. Against such things there is no law. Those who belong to Christ Jesus have crucified the flesh with its passions and desires. Since we live by the Spirit, let us keep in step with the Spirit. Let us not become conceited, provoking and envying each other. (Galatians 5:22–26)*

Couples meditate on this Scripture for two days, and ask the Lord: "How can I apply this Scripture in our relationship?" The wife is asking for her husband to be more patient with her. She is open to change, and her husband is open to change. God may bring change into her life by helping her to be more self-controlled or faithful to understand how to prioritize certain purchases for their family.

God may bring change to the man by helping him to be more gentle and trusting toward his wife as she purchases things that he may not feel are priorities. He may be too controlling when it comes to finances. As the husband embraces the changes that God desires to make in his life, their relationship becomes more Christ-like. The same is true for the wife, who embraces the changes that God brings into her life. Each person is a catalyst of change for their relationship.

### Reconciliation Stage

The Reconciliation stage points couples toward their future. Couples who believe that the best is yet ahead are more likely to embrace opportunities for change. However, men or women who think that change is about recapturing the past have missed the purpose of change. There is little hope in trying to recapture the past, even if it is filled with better memories. Maturity comes with moving toward the future, not in trying to recapture the past.

Couples who understand the power of change are willing to experience losses in order to reap the benefits of change. This principle is true for most circumstances. Someone who wants to lose weight must be willing to experience the loss of eating pastries or McDonald's fries. The loss is worth the benefit of losing weight. The same is true for relationships. Couples who are willing to make things better for their spouse must be willing to suffer some loss of their personal preferences, hobbies or goals. However, the best is yet ahead, because they will become more like Jesus and their relationship will be filled with the blessings of God.

## Resolving Conflict

*"Conflict is inevitable, but combat is optional."* – Max Lucado

The five styles of conflict resolution include *competing, compromise, collaboration, accommodating* and *avoidance* (Kilmann, 2009). Couples who agree to a collaborative style of conflict resolution will serve as change agents in their relationships. Collaboration is a commitment to understand the problem from the other person's perspective. The other four styles of conflict resolution are linear approaches to conflict resolution.

1. *Competing* is also described as an "I win, you lose" scenario of conflict resolution.
2. *Compromising* is also known as an "I win, then you can win" scenario of conflict resolution.
3. *Collaborating* is also known as a "we both win" scenario. This is the preferred model of conflict resolution.
4. *Accommodating* is also known as an "I win, when you are happy with me" scenario of conflict resolution
5. *Avoiding* is also known as a "you win, I always lose" scenario of conflict resolution.

A collaborative style of conflict resolution or circularity allows someone to see how they contribute to the conflict, even when they are unaware of an offense that the other person holds. Circularity is not limited to a specific beginning or end to conflict in the relationship.

Conflict has many processes of engagement and is usually connected to other issues.

By contrast, linear thinking views the other person as responsible for the conflict. This type of process eliminates one person from any possible responsibility for an offense.

The following guidelines will equip couples to develop a collaborative style of conflict resolution:

1. Rate the intensity of the conflict on a scale of one to five.

2. Conflicts that are at level one or two can be scheduled at a convenient time for both people. These types of conflict do not need immediate attention.

3. Conflicts that receive a three or four rating must be addressed quickly and prioritized by:
   - Setting a date to discuss the conflict.
   - Setting a time limit on the discussion (approximately 30 minutes). If the conflict cannot be resolved within this time, another date and time must be agreed on before the conversation ends.
   - Setting the location for the meeting (home, coffee shop, or an agreed location).
   - Each person must take time to identify how and what is affecting them in a negative way.
   - Each person must present solutions to the problem and suggestions on how to resolve the conflict.
   - Couples must follow the two-question format for resolving conflicts: *"What do you want to be different about …?"* And: *"How can I make it better for you?"*
   - The person who is offended must be able to communicate what triggered the offense.

4. A five rating on the intensity scale should rarely happen unless there is a crisis event, such as an affair or hidden debt. Couples need to consult a third party (pastor or counselor) when the intensity is at this level.

The LIMRI worksheets enable couples to engage in the Change Process and the five steps of conflict resolution. The Patience Worksheet in Appendix F will help couples work on this particular aspect of their relationship. Couples that use a collaborative conflict resolution style understand that both of them are embracing an opportunity to make things better for each other in order to enrich their relationship.

**Part II**

# Regression from Oneness

# CHAPTER TEN

# The Regression from Oneness Model

The remainder of this book will focus on a restorative model of marriage relationships. Over the last twenty years, many couples have said:

- "Our premarital relationship did not include the type of values that are found in the Journey to Oneness."
- "I didn't know my identity in Christ before I was married."
- "We haven't acted like friends for a long time."

My response is: You can create new pathways of friendship and shared values by following the LIMRI growth plans. These growth plans will give you spiritual and practical applications to renew friendship and develop shared values.

Restoration does not happen by recapturing the early years of your marriage. Couples need to be reconciled to God and learn how to restore trust, respect and faithfulness in their relationship. The Regression from Oneness helps spouses to identify which of the stages of regression best represent their sliding away from oneness as they respond to the devastating effects of detached or disjointed relationships. Marriages do not fail on their own. One or both spouses fail to fulfill their responsibilities to honor their vows to each other.

## The Regression from Oneness

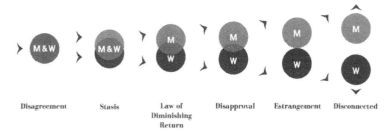

| Disagreement | Stasis | Law of Diminishing Return | Disapproval | Estrangement | Disconnected |

**Regression from Oneness Model**

The Regression from Oneness is the antithesis of the Journey to Oneness. The diagram above describes the six stages through which couples slide away from oneness into being disconnected.

Couples will feel more disconnected from each other as they slide deeper into the stages of regression. The Regression from Oneness helps couples to pinpoint the consequences of harmful or sinful behavior that have pulled them away from one another.

### *Disjointed Relationships*

Crisis events such as infidelity (physical or emotional), hidden debt, domestic abuse, pornography, sex addictions or emotional affairs create what I call a "disjointed" couple. These events pull a couple away from one another in ways that are similar to a separated shoulder. The arm is pulled away from the joint with such force that it becomes separated from the shoulder socket. The separation creates intense pain that throws the whole body into shock, and the shoulder can no longer support the weight of the arm.

There are many similarities between a separated shoulder and a crisis marriage. The offending spouse becomes trapped in the snare of sin because of their rebellion against God and the marriage covenant.

> *It has been said: "Sin will cost you more than you wanted to pay and keep you longer than you wanted to stay." Sinful behavior*

*stings and increases the longer a spouse remains in its grasp. As a result, the disjointed couple suffers a double wound.*

In disjoined relationships, an offending spouse is caught in a painful trap, while the offended spouse struggles to overcome the consequences of the sinful behavior. In many ways, the innocent spouse has a greater burden to bear because he/she did nothing to bring the sinful consequences into the marriage. The first step toward reconciliation occurs when the offended spouse seeks help from a pastor or counselor to address the painful consequences of betrayal. An offended spouse needs to take an appropriate amount of time to heal before entering into a process of reconciliation.

### Detached Relationships

The following is an illustration of a detached couple:

*Deborah and Charles have been struggling to feel connected to each other for quite some time. Deborah was expecting Charles to be home at a certain time, but he was on the opposite side of town with a client. She calls him on his cell phone to ask why he is so late for dinner.*

*Deborah and Charles are not listening to each other. They want to be understood rather than hear things from their spouse's perspective. To compound the problem, their connection has a lot of static, making it more difficult for either of them to be heard. It doesn't take long for them to start talking over each other because of the poor connection. The emotional intensity increases as each person is frustrated when they feel interrupted or misunderstood.*

*After repeated attempts to communicate their side of things, Deborah and Charles become so frustrated that they stop communicating altogether. In essence, they give up, believing the other person is no longer interested in listening to what they have to say.*

Often, a detached couple will limit their conversations to topics that are safe, such as the children's needs, household maintenance or vacations. They no longer attempt to communicate about anything related to issues of the heart or personal needs. Rarely do they talk about their devotional lives, fears, or what brings them joy. Couples can be trapped in detached relationships for many years, but eventually, there will be a tipping point and the relationship will escalate into a crisis.

In detached relationships, both people are guilty of withholding love from one another. In counseling, couples will say things like: "I used to show lots of empathy, encouragement or support, but it was never received, so I stopped expressing these things to my spouse."

In Luke 6:27–28, Jesus teaches an invaluable lesson for life as well as marriage when he says:

*"But I say to you who hear: Love your enemies, do good to those who hate you, bless those who curse you, and pray for those who spitefully use you." (NKJV)*

This Scripture reveals the priority of the kingdom of God – of love over self-protection and self-preservation. Most people will say that loving your enemies is nearly impossible. The good news is that most people do not have a list of true enemies, as defined as someone who wants to destroy or kill them. So, even though this command is not something that is required on a regular basis, the heart of every believer is to lean toward fulfilling it when presented with an opportunity.

The second command is to bless those who curse you. You will find more opportunities to practice this command, because there are more opportunities to interact with people who would speak poorly of you, such as coworkers, neighbors or family members.

The last command, to pray for the people who spitefully use you, is widely applicable, because many people in this world will take advantage of you.

As followers of Jesus, we must be willing to fulfill these commands in order to model the kingdom of light to the world so that our enemies, slanderers and persecutors will experience the grace and mercy of God. If we are commanded to treat enemies, persecutors and slanderers in this way, how much more are we commanded to love our spouse in the same way? Who could ever claim an exemption from loving their spouse? This is why I say that all spouses, in some capacity, are guilty of withholding love from their husband/wife and will have many opportunities to repent to one another.

## Disagreement

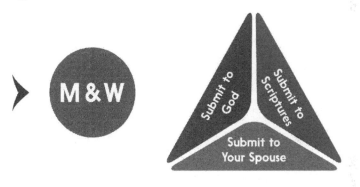

**Stage I: Disagreement**

The first stage in the Regression from Oneness is Disagreement. The disagreement that forms in a crisis marriage is the antithesis of Blessing as described in the Journey to Oneness. The blessing comes from a spouse's commitment to submit to God, the Scriptures and each other. Disagreement forms in the relationship when one or both spouses refuse to submit their lives to God or one another.

The marriage covenant brings two people into an agreement, while sinful behavior and attitudes create disagreement in your relationship. One spouse is caught in rebellious behaviors such as infidelity, an emotional affair, lies, hidden debt or pornography, while the unsuspecting spouse feels locked out of their husband/wife's heart due to hiding these types of rebellious choices.

### Disagreement over God's Authority

Couples in this stage of regression are missing the peace and unity that comes from knowing that each person is walking in a healthy fear of the Lord. Sinful behaviors are rooted in rebellion against God. The spouse who is caught in these types of behaviors are making a statement, "I will decide what is best and good for me." As followers of Jesus, we must be willing to submit to God's authority and his holiness over our lives.

### Disagreement over the Scriptures

Couples in this stage no longer seek wisdom from the Scriptures. The Bible is no longer their compass that directs their moral, social, and family values. Spouses will seek out other wisdom and counsel to justify their behavior or values.

### Disagreement over Mutual Submission

Couples in this stage no longer benefit from mutual accountability. Spouses understand each other better than anyone else and know each other's areas of weakness and growth. Whenever mutual accountability is lost, spouses will become stuck in patterns of behavior that are embedded in their broken humanity. Spouses need the encouragement and commitment that their husband/wife extends to them in order to keep these types of behavior in check. For example:

- The husband struggles to limit his drinking at social events. His wife holds him accountable to a two-drink limit.
- The wife struggles to stay within the family budget. Her husband holds her accountable for her spending habits.

A crisis has developed in their relationship because of an unwillingness to submit their lives, choices and behavior to the Lord and his Word. The relationship is now struggling with a disagreement over the authority of the Lord in their personal lives and marriage. No longer is the relationship centered on Jesus and the Scriptures.

The Disagreement stage leads to a stasis in the relationship. Stasis forms in a relationship when spouses disagree over the authority of God, Scriptures and mutual submission in their marriage.

## Stasis

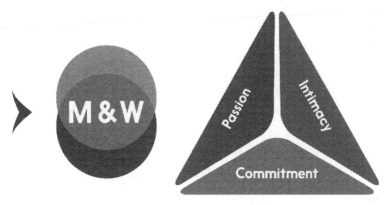

**Stage II: Stasis**

The diagram above shows the arrow pointing in the opposite direction of oneness. A crisis event stops the forward progress of the marriage and sends the couple cascading deeper into the stages of regression.

*Stasis* is a word that describes a state or condition in which no action or progress is taking place, like a state of suspended animation. Suspended animation might have benefits in space travel, but not in a relationship. A stasis occurs when one spouse refuses to repent when confronted or continues in hidden sinful behaviors. The other spouse may be unsuspecting of these hidden sins or unwilling to hold them accountable. In essence, they are both affected by stasis. Relationships cannot grow because of sinful patterns like these, whether hidden for years or newly discovered.

Even though a controlled stasis would make space travel to distant galaxies a possibility for astronauts, they would be powerless to respond to emergencies that occur during their journey. The same thing can happen to crisis couples. Even though the system-failure light has been flashing for a number of months or years, the couple has slipped into a type of suspended animation and they are powerless to make adjustments that could turn their relationship toward oneness again.

One of the first cause and effects of stasis is a push toward independence rather than interdependence. Independence disconnects spouses emotionally and spiritually from one another. A detached couple will eventually push each other into the peripheral areas of their lives by limiting conversations to topics like work, home maintenance and children's activities. At this point, each spouse protects his/her heart from being disappointed and is unwilling to engage spiritually or emotionally with each other.

## Stasis of Commitment

Commitment, like faith, is either increasing or decreasing in measure and practice. A detached or disjointed couple must guard their hearts against forming negative sentiments toward each other. A negative sentiment becomes evident when spouses make statements like:

- "You never listen to what I say."
- "You never think about my needs."
- "You always put your needs above mine."

When this happens, a couple will find themselves on opposite ends of conflict resolution. One will be on the defensive, while the other is on the offensive. Couples who become trapped in negative sentiments are powerless to initiate change in their relationship because neither is listening and both spouses only want to be heard. As soon as one of them says "you always" or "you never", their spouse stops listening to the conversation.

## Stasis of Intimacy

Intimacy is best described as fidelity. Couples who vow to be faithful to each other are committed to put their spouse's needs above his/her own preferences or needs. The characteristic of fidelity means that couples are committed to love one another more than all other people, possessions or personal goals. Couples who are caught in stasis receive more positive feedback from coworkers, friends and extended family members than they do from their spouse.

## Stasis of Passion (Physical Intimacy)

In Stage V (Marriage Covenant) of the Journey to Oneness, couples celebrate receiving each other's body as a gift from God. The gift of physical intimacy is joined with the other seventeen characteristics that define the marriage covenant. One of the ways couples celebrate their marriage covenant is through physical intimacy.

*The stasis of emotional and physical intimacy turns the outward focus of what is best for your spouse into the selfish expressions of what is best for me.*

The marriage covenant requires couples not only to share their bodies, but also to be aware of each other's sexual and emotional needs. A prolonged stasis in the relationship creates suspicion about their spouse's commitment to sexual fidelity and emotional intimacy.

*Selfish desires reduce lovemaking to sexual acts. Sexual performance replaces physical and emotional intimacy. Couples who fall into the "performance trap" will leave the bedroom wondering, "Is this all I have to look forward to?" Sexual performance only benefits couples at the moment of orgasm. However, sexual intimacy enriches marriage relationships beyond the bedroom.*

Couples in Stage II will struggle with the effects of entropy. *Entropy* is the second law of thermodynamics and describes a decreasing measure of energy in a physical system that no longer can sustain itself. In a relationship, entropy occurs when spouses are pulling in opposite directions. A couple can change the trajectory of their relationship by extending grace and mercy toward one another. A relationship without grace and mercy suffers from the damaging effects of ambivalence.

*Ambivalence* is a simultaneous and contradictory attitude or feeling toward a person (Merriam-Webster, 2011). These types of attitudes or feelings seep into relationships when two conflicting emotions are directed at the same person, such as love and hate, or trust and control. Couples may love each other, but hate how their husband/ wife treats them with contempt when he/she asks for changes in the relationship. Ambivalence has devastating effects on the hearts of the rebellious man or woman and their spouse:

- An offending spouse will struggle with ambivalence when forgiveness is withheld after they confess, repent and demonstrate a willingness to restore trust.
- An offended spouse will struggle with ambivalence when they extend forgiveness, but their husband/wife maintains the sin pattern. The offended spouse will often struggle with shame and guilt for allowing themselves to be subjected to such harmful behavior.

Couples who find themselves in the Stasis stage will quickly fall into survival mode rather than making changes to enrich their relationship. Individually, they will exhaust all their emotional and spiritual resources trying to make their relationship better but, unfortunately, they will find that each day exhausts all their reserves of trust and hope. At this stage, spouses pull in opposite directions in search of some type of stability in the midst of the chaos that surrounds their relationship. Any remaining energy is invested outside their marriage relationship such as parenting, careers and hobbies. These types of diversions create a sense of significance and security that gives momentary relief from their struggling marriage.

Spouses who disregard the values of faith, nurture and family life will not be trusted with something as intimate as the body of their mate. Couples who ignore the stasis of passion in their relationship will not be able to avoid sliding into Stage III (Law of Diminished Return) in the Regression from Oneness. The stages of Disagreement and Stasis can be undetected in a relationship for quite a while. But Stage III makes a greater negative impact on the relationship.

# CHAPTER ELEVEN

# Law of Diminished Return and Disapproval

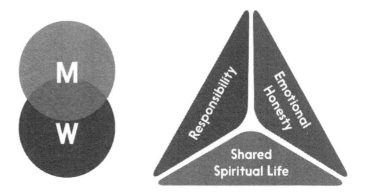

**Stage III: Law of Diminished Return**

## The Law of Diminished Return (Push)

The diagram above shows the loss of synergy in a relationship that is dealing with sins like domestic abuse, infidelity or hidden debt. The consequences of these types of sin pull couples away from each other. A couple suffering from these types of sinful behaviors no longer has the capacity to resolve conflicts. The foundational values of their marriage are affected by broken trust at the very core of their marriage covenant.

In this stage, spouses find themselves living out a scenario that is similar to the movie, *Groundhog Day*. In this movie, a man is caught in a repetitive cycle of living out the same daily events over and over again. Couples who slide into the Law of Diminished Return will grow weary of reliving the same disagreements or conflicts without ever coming to a resolution.

## How Negative Polarities Work against Relationships

Couples who find themselves in this stage are like two magnets that are being forced together. As children, playing with magnets taught us that two negative polarities cannot form a connection. You can actually feel the resistance building as you force them together. Spouses in this stage hear more negative than positive comments from each other, and will experience the same type of resistance. Spouses will feel the resistance building between them as they try to connect emotionally and spiritually with each other because they have become disjointed and detached. A negative sentiment forms in a relationship when couples are consumed with negative emotions and memories about their spouse.

*Couples forming negative sentiments toward one another will feel the intensity of their emotions escalating quickly whenever they try to talk to one another. These negative sentiments (polarity) keep them from connecting with each other as they try to resolve conflicts. Spouses can reconnect with each when one person is willing to flip his or her polarity from negative to positive.*

Spouses who extend grace, peace and mercy toward their husband/ wife who is struggling with emotions such as anger, shame or guilt will discover that these attributes allow them to reconnect and find help for their relationship.

### How Positive Polarities Work against Each Other

The same principle is true for relationships that are set in positive polarities. The spouse represents him/herself as being a good person, and resists any discussion about how they offend each other. The resistance increases as spouses interact with each other. Neither person will take responsibility for any offensive behavior or attitudes. A spouse who refuses to admit any shortcoming no longer sees any value in confessing his/her sins or seeking forgiveness. They view themselves only in the positive, and are unwilling to see how their behavior or attitudes contribute to a conflict. The other spouse is totally responsible for any unresolved conflicts.

### Positive and Negative Polarities Working Together

Spouses who embrace the realities of their sinful nature and redeemed humanity will be drawn toward one another. The "pull" toward each other is created when forgiveness meets repentance. Marriages, like magnets, need the positive and negative polarities to work together in order to form a shared identity. A shared identity allows couples to pull together and move in the direction of reconciliation.

An offending person who asks for forgiveness without making a commitment to repent and rebuild trust is taking advantage of her/his spouse. The spouse who receives forgiveness must be willing to do whatever it takes to overcome the sin pattern. For example, someone who abuses alcohol needs to join a support group to demonstrate repentance and that they are not taking advantage of the grace and mercy that is being extended to them (positive polarities).

### Loss of Responsibility

The loss of responsibility means that couples no longer volunteer to use their gifts, talents or available time to lighten the loads of their spouse. The couple begins to feel alone rather than like teammates in completing all their personal and family responsibilities.

Marriage relationships are filled with many opportunities for couples to serve one another. Life is full of responsibilities that require your time and attention, like bill paying, grocery shopping, cooking meals, mowing the lawn, changing a baby's diaper or fixing a leaky sink. These responsibilities are necessary to make life orderly, but they are far from representing your destiny and purpose in life.

The Builder Generation of the 1950s defined the roles and responsibilities of husbands and wives that still influence relationships in the New Millennium. Wives were expected to manage life inside the home, while husbands worked and managed life outside the home. Today couples need to look beyond what the Builders set up as norms for marriage relationships and move past the traditional markers of marriage relationships by sharing in the household responsibilities. This happens best when spouses assess their skills, interests and availability to fulfill tasks and chores in order to work as teammates on a winning team.

The number of couples where both spouses now work outside of the home has dramatically increased. They need to support one another after long days on the job. Couples with children do not have the luxury of going home to relax. They will find that working together to fulfill their parenting and home management responsibilities will develop closeness and appreciation for each other.

These types of roles and responsibilities fall short of defining someone's identity and value as a follower of Jesus. God did not create men to ensure that cars, sinks and lawn mowers function properly. Nor did he create women for the sole purpose of doing all the domestic chores, like the cooking, cleaning or shopping. Men and women need to be faithful and diligent to complete these domestic responsibilities and champion each other as unique, unrepeatable miracles of God.

## Avoiding Negative Sentiment in Relationships

My wife is meticulous about the way she decorates our home and she always receives compliments from our visitors. Her attention to detail became widely known, even to our children's friends. Our children and their friends would turn pictures or knickknacks one-eighth of an inch, then sit back and watch Barbara walk directly to the item and correct its position. Sometimes they would rearrange the fruit bowl and howl with laughter when she discovered the apples and oranges were in the wrong order.

I greatly appreciate the way my wife organizes our home. Her attention to detail and cleanliness blesses our family. But, whenever I was frustrated with Barbara, I would focus on the disorderly closet. The house would look great, but I would look at what was not done and focus on those things. The house can be meticulously clean, but the disorderly closet gets the attention of the disgruntled spouse. Negative sentiments find fault with someone or something – no matter how well things are done. Whenever negativity creeps into relationships, faultfinding becomes the norm. A negative spouse will look past the positive things in order to find something to criticize.

Barbara also had to choose against developing a negative sentiment toward me when I remodeled the kitchen and bathroom in our home. If she had evaluated my abilities based on the speed and timeliness of these projects, I would have come up short in comparison to other husbands, who are more gifted in these areas. I can accomplish most household projects, but it usually takes me much longer than anticipated and costs twice the projected budget, because I break things! She had to wait a long time for a remodeled kitchen and bathroom. Barbara has to guard her heart to keep herself from looking at my skills negatively.

Couples that struggle with diminished viewpoints or negative sentiments will say things like:

- "She is a great wife, but … her cooking or cleaning is lacking."

- "He's very organized but … he can't replace a light bulb or fix a leaky sink."

Before couples enter the Regression from Oneness, they usually take personal responsibility for their offenses. Whenever one person fails to honor his/her agreements, they quickly repent of their failure, and the offended spouse is quick to forgive. But spouses who find themselves in Stage III commonly say things like:

- "You only did that because you wanted something from me."
- "You only bought that for me because you wanted to buy something for yourself."

### Protecting Your Relationship

Spouses can safeguard their relationship from the Law of Diminished Return by ensuring that home management and maintenance is divided equitably rather than according to traditional, cultural or spiritual roles that can raise unrealistic expectations between husbands and wives. A couple typically goes about their daily activities trying to accomplish whatever items are on their chore list, and by the end of the week or month, when everything needs to be evaluated, they may be asking each other:

- "Did *you* clean the garage?"
- "Did *you* balance the checkbook?"
- "Did *you* get the steaks for the picnic?"

If the answer is "no" to any of these questions, something needs to change. It may indicate that a couple is working too independently from one another. I encourage couples to work interdependently in the areas of family management and home maintenance. Many husbands do not fix or repair things well and many wives do not excel with cooking or cleaning responsibilities. Couples will find that working together in many of these areas creates teamwork and develops appreciation for one another.

Interdependent relationships can minimize the disorderliness and chaos that comes with busy lives and hectic schedules. Couples who make checklists of their weekly responsibilities can volunteer to complete them according to their schedules, skills, interests and availability. Working together will lighten the load of their spouse and develop deeper appreciation for one another.

### Loss of Emotional Honesty

Couples in this stage are no longer able to disagree with each other and remain respectful. The loss of emotional honesty is like a solvent that removes the glue that holds two objects together. One of the strengths of a marriage is the ability of two spouses to disagree and not feel threatened by the different viewpoints of the other. A couple that has an emotionally honest relationship truly believes that their spouse will have his/her best interest in mind. When this characteristic is missing, a spouse begins to doubt their spouse's commitment to the relationship.

Couples who experience a loss of emotional honesty will rarely compliment each other's appearance or express appreciation for the little things they do for each other, like taking out the trash or cleaning the bathroom.

In Stage III of the Journey to Oneness, couples learn that "you can have a problem without being identified as being a problem". In the Regression from Oneness, *the person and the problem become linked together.* Couples will lose any synergy that was developed earlier in their relationships. Synergy works like this: A single horse can pull its own weight, while two horses pulling together create up to five horsepower. Couples in this third stage of regression will struggle to complete everyday tasks because of the loss of synergy.

> *Emotional honesty is lost when spouses look at each other as problems rather than as advocates. Spouses are responsible to challenge each other's viewpoints in order to see beyond their own biases, but also to defer to each other whenever possible.*

## Loss of a Shared Spiritual Life

The loss of a shared spiritual life means that spouses begin to privatize their faith. A couple in this stage begins to discuss their spiritual and emotional needs and prayer requests with friends or family members rather than his/her spouse. Once this pattern has developed, the couple begins to withhold other elements of their personal life from their spouse.

Another casualty of sliding into the Law of Diminished Return involves couples disengaging from their practice of the spiritual disciplines. Prayers become requests for God to fix what is wrong with their spouse rather than speaking a blessing over one another. A prayer from a diminished spiritual life sounds like this: "God, what are you going to do about my spouse?" A better prayer is: "Please heal the gap between us. Use me to model love and mercy in our relationship."

Couples in this stage no longer believe they can make a difference in their relationship. During the premarital process, couples had to address questions such as:

- "Am I committed to be a gift to my future spouse?"
- "Am I prepared to receive him/her as a gift from you?"

At this stage of regression, couples rarely see their spouse as a gift from God.

Couples who want to reestablish a shared spiritual life must begin to practice the spiritual disciplines together. Couples need to make commitments to bring God's blessings of love, hope and grace into their relationship. Spiritual disciplines lead to obedience to God and his Word. Couples can begin to reestablish spiritual disciplines by completing their LIMRI worksheets (see Praying with Each Other Worksheet in Appendix G).

### Can You Change the Direction of a Crisis Marriage?

In order for couples to change the direction of a crisis marriage, they must stop sliding further into the other stages of regression. The offending spouse must confess and repent, and demonstrate the fruit of repentance in ways that show they are becoming accountable to their husband/wife for their schedules, leisure time, email, social media, spending habits and phone records, etc.

The offended spouse will often withdraw emotionally, physically and spiritually from their husband/wife in search of relief from the betrayal associated with infidelity, an emotional affair, drug/alcohol abuse, hidden debt, or physical and emotional abuse.

These behaviors can have long-term consequences on the soul of the offended spouse. But if the offending spouse confesses, repents and seeks forgiveness, they can begin the healing process for the spouse who is struggling with the loss of trust, respect and faithfulness.

The offended and offending spouses need to avoid sliding deeper into the further stages of regression. Each person needs to focus on their personal relationship with God to seek forgiveness for the offenses and healing for being sinned against. These responses stop couples from transitioning to the next stage of regression.

### Can Every Marriage Be Reconciled?

I firmly believe that crisis marriages can be reconciled. However, divorce is allowed over patterns of sinful behavior such as infidelity, abandonment, withholding conjugal love, withdrawing emotional support, financial irresponsibility or domestic violence. These sins are not a death sentence for a marriage, even though these types of behavior do meet the biblical guidelines for divorce. I believe that the greatest enemy of marriage is a hardening of the heart by an offending spouse.

I define a *hardness of heart* as an unwillingness to submit to God, the Scriptures, the authority of the church and one's spouse.

Marriage is important to God. That is why Jesus said: "What God has joined together, let no one separate" (Matthew 19:6). I firmly believe that covenant relationships have all the resources of heaven available to them. Couples who choose to submit, confess, repent, demonstrate the fruit of repentance and forgive each other can experience reconciliation.

I see too many couples choosing to end their marriage based on misguided belief systems that are summed up by these two statements:

- "I must have married the wrong person."
- "The right one is still out there."

These misguided viewpoints are contrary to the ministry of reconciliation.

> *God gave his church the ministry of reconciliation, because he knew we would desperately need it (2 Corinthians 5:18). Reconciliation sets the church apart from all other types or organizations or institutions. Our lives are not defined by our sinful behavior or the consequences of being sinned against, because we have been reconciled to God through Christ Jesus.*

## Swiss Cheese

Spouses who push or pull away from one another will discover many holes in each other's character. These holes resemble a block of Swiss cheese. The holes in the block of cheese make it unique but, as the deli slicer cuts the block into thinner slices, the holes become more pronounced. In some cases, it appears as if there are more holes than cheese, and the thinner it is sliced, the more noticeable the holes become.

As spouses become detached emotionally and spiritually, they begin to notice the gaps (holes) in each other's values, integrity or honesty. Marriage joins a couple together in holy matrimony, but wedding ceremonies do not make them complete. A spouse's struggle with any of these negative bents, or "holes," can be covered by their partner's positive bents, represented by the gifts and fruit of the Holy Spirit. It is always amazing to see how one spouse is able to complement the underdeveloped areas of the husband or wife's character or abilities.

Loneliness and isolation cause couples to slide deeper into the stages of regression. Couples who are struggling in these ways believe that disconnecting emotionally and spiritually from their irresponsible or unrepentant spouses will limit the chaos that is created by sinful behavior and attitudes. For the majority of spouses who pull away from each other for reasons outside of safety concerns or illegal activities, this will propel them into the next stage of regression, Stage IV, Disapproval.

*Discussion Questions*

1. In what role or area of responsibility do you feel your spouse expresses a diminished viewpoint of you?
2. Identify areas where you have a diminished viewpoint of your spouse.
3. What responsibilities or roles would you want to change in your relationship?
4. What can you do to change your viewpoint of or attitude toward your spouse?

## Disapproval

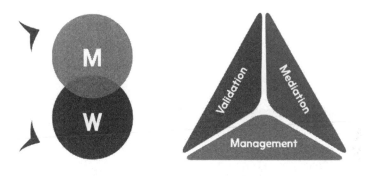

**Stage IV: Disapproval**

Disapproval is the antithesis of validation, as described in the Journey to Oneness. Validation is all about accepting someone as a unique, unrepeatable miracle of God. Each person is God's child created to express love, grace, mercy and justice to everyone they meet. Disapproval is refusing to acknowledge someone's value to God and as a spouse or parent.

A couple in this stage rarely views their spouse in the same way God sees them. Because of being detached or disjointed, couples usually view their spouse through the lens of broken trust and the sins that have harmed their marriage.

In order to avoid further wounding, spouses may choose to say nothing when they disagree with each other, but saying nothing actually shows disapproval toward one's spouse. Spouses will feel as if their husband/wife is stonewalling them rather than trying to avoid escalation. Silence is one of the greatest enemies of a relationship. Even though one spouse may feel that not saying anything rather than something hurtful is better for the relationship, they are actually causing more harm than good. The other spouse will fill in the silence with things like: "My spouse doesn't love me, respect me or trust me." Silence does not help the struggling relationship.

Spouses should not use disrespectful or disingenuous language to discuss difficult areas of their relationship. In order to break the pattern of disapproval and reestablish validation, a couple needs to:

- Speak the truth with love (Ephesians 4:15) by learning to communicate their commitment to one another before they address difficult topics.
- Encourage one another to do good works (Titus 3:8) by serving others through the local church.
- Stay connected to a small group in order to avoid isolation (Hebrews 10:25).

In order to stop the process of disapproval in relationships, a couple also needs to:

- Believe the best about who they are in Christ (2 Corinthians 5:17).
- Know that each person is a sinner saved by grace (Romans 3:23).
- Remember that God knows the heart and intercedes for them (Romans 8:26).
- Stop judging (Luke 6:37).
- Call on Jesus as their high priest who understands their trials and tribulation. He is able to empathize, comfort and empower them to overcome sin and temptation (Hebrews 2:14–18; 4:14–16).

# CHAPTER TWELVE

# From Estrangement to Disconnection

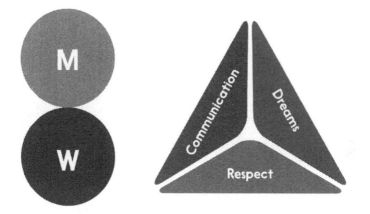

**Stage V: Estrangement**

The diagram above shows two circles nearly separated from one another. Couples in this stage of regression become silent as they grieve the loss of friendship in their marriage.

This loss is best described by someone who is visiting their hometown after being away for many years. The buildings, streets and playgrounds are all familiar, but the relationships are missing. You feel like a visitor in your own hometown. The same thing happens to spouses when they lose their friendship with each other. A husband and wife share a house, but it no longer feels like a home. Couples in the Estrangement stage feel detached in the areas of communication, dreams and respect.

### Estrangement of Communication

Spouses who once excelled in communication now try to end their conversations with each other as quickly as possible. The kind and playful words that friends regularly share with each other have been replaced with sharp, irritable and finger-pointing accusations.

As soon as their eyes meet, their hearts are filled with negative emotions like anger or rejection. At one time, a simple glance at each other would fill their hearts with love and encouragement, but now they feel as if they have been robbed of respect, encouragement and peace.

### Estrangement of Dreams

They no longer discuss the shared dreams that once represented a hope-filled future for them. At one time, their future was full of possibilities, but now these dreams only represent a distant memory of their past. Any pursuit of goals is now interpreted as a selfish expression of independence. Spouses in this stage will blame each other for blocking or limiting the fulfillment of their personal dreams and goals.

### Estrangement of Respect

A benevolent attitude or acts of returned honor are no long commonplace between spouses. At this stage of regression, some spouses will make only their half of the bed or wash their dinner dishes and leave everything else in the sink. At one time, their relationship was blessed by acts of kindness, but now the attitude toward marriage is summed up by the statement, "What's in it for me?" Couples in Stage V rarely talk about sharing dreams or activities with their spouse. Conversations may sound like this:

- "I'm going to take some college courses so that I have a few more options in my future."
- "I'm going to start collecting antiques or sports cards, or working out, etc."

Spouses must stop the slide of regression before irreparable damage happens to their relationship. They must do everything possible to guard their friendship, because true friends are hard to come by, and the loss of friendship leaves a deep wound.

*A true friend is a rare commodity. Proverbs 18:24 reveals that someone with many friends will be unable to serve them all faithfully and will lead to your downfall, but there is a friend who is closer than a brother. Your spouse is this type of friend who adds value to your life.*

The first step in recapturing friendship is to seek out what it means to be a friend of God. I believe that friendship is the highest expression of discipleship. Jesus said: "I have called you friends" (John 15:15). Recapturing friendship with Jesus will allow a husband and a wife to reinvest in the friendship they desire with each other. Faithfulness and friendship go hand in hand by:

- Being faithful to God.
- Being faithful to your marriage covenant.
- Being faithful to your family values.

## Disconnected

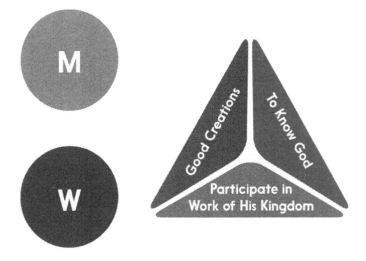

**Stage VI: Disconnected**

The diagram above shows the last stage in the regression from oneness. The circles (couple) are no longer touching each other. Couples who become disconnected from their spiritual identities and purpose in life will feel cut-off from their spouse emotionally and spiritually. A disconnected couple shares only a few of the characteristics of oneness in their marriage relationship. This type of relationship can be reconciled, but spouses must seek the help of a pastor or professional Christian counselor.

## Tough Questions

Couples in this stage may begin to wrestle with some tough questions about their marriage.

## Did I Marry the Wrong Person?

Couples in Stage III in the Regression from Oneness ask the question: "Did I marry the wrong person?" This is a dangerous question for spouses who are in a detached or disjointed relationship. A couple who remains in this stage for a few months will feel uncomfortable trying to pull in the same direction as their spouse, and may begin to think that life as a single adult would be less chaotic and stressful than staying married.

Conventional wisdom leads spouses to believe that, if they picked the wrong partner, the right one must still be available. This belief leads to two wrong conclusions. The first is stated like this: "I chose poorly, so I am destined to be punished for the rest of my life because my marriage was a mistake." The second conclusion leads spouses to consider getting a divorce in hopes of finding the "right" person. These questions suggest that life as a single adult would be less chaotic than staying married. Couples must seek a biblical response to the question: "Did I marry the wrong person?"

I am arguing against both of these conclusions, because God has foreknowledge of all things and is able to work all things together for the good to those who are called according to his purposes (Romans 8:28–30). With this understanding of the Scriptures, I believe you *become* the right person for one another as you submit your lives to Christ and to one another. Therefore, I do not believe you marry the wrong person rather than the right person. God does not desire to punish you, nor should you punish yourself, but he does want you to be committed to your marriage.

In this stage of regression, trust is something that must be earned. The LIMRI worksheets will help couples to reestablish the values of emotional honesty, responsibility and a shared spiritual life in their relationship. These worksheets help couples to begin to pull in the same direction as they practice new ways of relating to each other.

*Whenever relationships become chaotic, reconciliation and restoration must be pursued, if at all possible, before someone chooses to separate or divorce. In cases of domestic violence, safety is the first priority.*

I have seen great animosity develop between spouses because one of them believes that they married the wrong person. When this happens, a couple will live independently from one another because they view their marriage as a liability rather than a blessing. No longer are they working together to enrich or restore their relationship. They become consumed with the question: "What is God's will for *me*?" rather than: "What is God's will for *our marriage*?"

## Shaking the Foundation

The type of disconnection in this stage is not physical but emotional and spiritual. A couple will experience a violent shaking of their core values and spiritual identity. In the book of Matthew, chapter 19, Jesus warns against social values that weaken the marriage covenant that God has created between husbands and wives. Simply put, marriage belongs to God.

At this point, each spouse is struggling in their relationship with God. I do not mean to say that a husband or a wife in this stage of regression does not have a loving relationship with God. On the contrary, as many spouses have said to me: "God's presence is the only thing sustaining me through this crisis in my marriage." A couple in this stage is thrust into survival mode as each day is filled with unmet marital expectations.

Spouses become disconnected due to unconfessed sin and broken trust. Whenever one spouse suggests marriage counseling, the other spouse becomes unwilling to accept their bid for reconciliation. The spouse who proposes reconciliation suffers humiliation and heartache with every rejection of their bids. In some cases, an offending spouse rejects these bids because they feel their husband/wife

deserves someone who will not hurt them. Instead of seeking reconciliation, they feel that divorce is the best option their spouse has to
have a better life. A bid is an invitation to connect and reestablish
hope for the relationship.

An offending spouse also becomes unreceptive to reconciliation as
a result of the overwhelming losses of intimacy, sacrificial love and
friendship with God and their spouse. A couple in this stage must
get help immediately to counteract the violence against their core
marriage identity as a "good creation" and God's purpose for them.

## Disconnected from being a "Good Creation"

In this stage, the idea of marriage as a good creation of God is threatened by deep feelings of loneliness between a husband and a wife.
Marriage is all about community, but broken trust pulls spouses
away from one another causing multiple fractures in their shared
identity. A fractured identity leaves each spouse feeling alone in their
own sorrow, emotional pain and suffering. They no longer feel as if
their marriage is a good creation of God, and hopelessness can set in
for both spouses.

## Disconnected from Knowing God's Holiness

Spouses who continue in their sin patterns begin to experience a
seared conscience and no longer experience God's presence. A seared
conscience leads to a hedonistic lifestyle that only desires momentary pleasures. The offended spouse is powerless to change what is
happening in their marriage. Most likely, they have made many
attempts (even to the point of emotional and spiritual exhaustion) to
make the marriage better, but all of their attempts fall short of their
expectations.

## Disconnected from Participating in the Work of the Kingdom

Marriage is a powerful representation of God's kingdom on Earth
and allows couples to serve as living examples of unconditional love

and faithfulness to one another. Couples in this stage are no longer able to invite others to follow them as they follow Jesus. In some cases, couples who serve as leaders in their church will need to step out of ministry in order to give full attention to their marriage and walk out the pathway of reconciliation.

Spouses in this stage need to rediscover what the Scriptures say about them as God's children. The following Scriptures will help couples to recapture their true identity and purpose:

- 1 Peter 2:9 – you are chosen by God and special to him.
- 2 Thessalonians 2:13 – you have been chosen for salvation.
- 2 Corinthians 1:3 – God desires to comfort and be merciful to you.

## Returning to Oneness

The return to oneness requires couples to own their sin and to seek healing from being sinned against. Reconciliation begins individually, rather than as a couple. The restoring of relationships comes later.

### The Performance Trap

*The early years of Maurice and Patricia's marriage were filled with love, encouragement and excitement about their future. As an engaged couple, they invested in premarital classes and marriage coaching in order to build a foundation that would allow them to overcome the trials and tribulations of living in a chaotic world.*

*Maurice and Patricia were overachievers in all things related to life and godliness. They had plans to start a family, and for career advancement while serving and leading in their local church and community. Each day was filled with opportunities to live out their dreams. Unfortunately, the pace of their lives distracted them from seeing the warning signs leading to a relationship crisis.*

For Maurice and Patricia, buying a home was a good investment. And a new car meant lower maintenance and fuel costs. As their children approached middle school, they chose to enroll them in private schools in order to give them an excellent academic program and strong spiritual foundation.

All of the good things that were happening in their lives began to drive their personal and financial decisions. At least four nights a week, they ate out at restaurants because it saved lots of time as they drove their children to sporting events, dance lessons and church activities. Weekends were full – they attended athletic games, recitals and extended family gatherings – but life was everything they had imagined it would be. The children were happy, and they were pursuing their goals, but their relationship began to suffer.

In order to turn things around, they tried to cut back on the number of weekly activities in order to prioritize their marriage and family life. Maurice decided to stop attending his men's group and Patricia had to drop out of the small group that she had coled for many years. Maurice did his best to get in a round of golf each week and Patricia joined a health club to be sure that she remained sharp, both physically and mentally.

The family expenses continued to increase with escalating fees for sports activities, dance classes, school tuition, vacations and new tax levies. The additional expenses began to put financial pressure on their marriage. Maurice and Patricia were rarely in the same car or at the same place all week long. Weekends were reserved for family, but even then, they were at separate activities making sure their kids were receiving parental support. Church attendance declined from a weekly investment to once or twice a month.

Maurice and Patricia had normal arguments, but they fell into a habit of skipping over one problem to deal with the next pressing issue. It was easy to blame their schedules for not having time to resolve conflicts or manage their finances.

*After a few years, they had accumulated thousands of dollars in credit card debt. The debt became too much to manage, so they began to make minimum payments rather than making a plan to change their spending habits. As Maurice and Patricia's debt grew, they became more detached and blamed each other for their financial mismanagement.*

*The push for success rather than faithful stewardship drove Maurice and Patricia further away from their shared values of faith and family life. Maurice would become testy when his favorite beverage was not in the refrigerator. Patricia became upset when her debit card wouldn't work because their account balances were too low. She would have to pull out the credit card to pay for day-to-day living expenses. Many of their conversations sounded like: "Why didn't you take care of …?" and: "How could you forget to get that done?"*

## Turning toward, Rather than away from, One Another

*Maurice and Patricia had little grace in their emotional tanks for one another. They finally made a decision to look inward rather than at each other's shortcomings. Maurice chose to extend grace and mercy toward Patricia in the area of home management, rather than looking for opportunities to criticize or blame her for unfulfilled responsibilities. Instead of being critical, he chose to encourage and offered his support.*

*Patricia chose to extend grace toward Maurice in the area of their finances. She was offended by Maurice's mismanagement of the family budget, but instead of judging him, she began to show encouragement and offered her support when needed.*

*Both of them began to own their personal responsibility for not offering solutions or holding each other accountable for mismanaging their personal lives and home responsibilities. Maurice and Patricia came to realize that they had allowed their circumstances rather than the Scriptures to serve as the foundation for their choices and decisions.*

*Maurice and Patricia experienced hope for their relationship as they made life less chaotic for each other.*

*In a few months, they realized that there were more successes than failures in the way they fulfilled their responsibilities. Whenever Maurice and Patricia failed to accomplish their tasks or responsibilities, they were willing to extend grace, mercy and encouragement toward each other. The consequences for neglecting their finances, home management and spiritual growth did not change overnight. It takes time and discipline to restore spiritual health and trust in these areas. Fortunately, Maurice and Patricia completely owned their mistakes.*

Spouses need to have realistic expectations for developing new patterns of behavior, and extend grace to cover any temporary setbacks when they fail to fulfill their responsibilities. One of the most positive things a couple could say about each other is: "I was encouraged to try harder as my spouse made our home an encouraging place."

## Discussion Questions

1. Discuss areas where you want to experience additional grace or mercy from your spouse.
2. Identify and discuss areas of mismanagement in your responsibilities of home management, maintenance or spiritual development.
3. Ask your spouse, "How can I be more encouraging to you?"
4. Identify one area of responsibility that you need to manage differently.
5. Ask your spouse, "What area of responsibility do you want me to manage differently?"
6. Make a commitment to become more accountable to your spouse in the area of your responsibilities, by asking the two questions:
   a. "What do you want to be different about …?"
   b. "How can I make it better for you?"

**Part III**

# The Journey Back to Oneness

# CHAPTER THIRTEEN

# Restoring a Marriage Relationship

The restoration of a marriage relationship requires couples to reestablish the values of fidelity, faith and family life. The two characteristics of a restored relationship are *rest* and *order*.

1. Rest creates a respite from the chaos of detached or disjointed relationships. Couples that reestablish the values of their covenant will no longer founder in the chaos of broken trust.
2. Order returns stability to the relationship as couples are accountable for their behaviors.

When couples put Jesus back in the center of their relationship, they recapture all that their marriage was meant to be. Restoration is a pilgrimage that starts with confession and repentance. These attributes lay the foundation of peace with God and with each other. Restoration allows spouses to celebrate the work of Christ in their lives and marriage.

Author Gary Thomas says: "Marriage is to make you holy, not happy." I believe that holiness comes as a result of inviting the Lord's love and grace into your life. Couples can experience his love and grace by praying in this way: "Father, I invite your love into my life and I receive you grace and mercy. Thank you for loving me as your child." People cannot become holy through traditions or religious works, but they can receive the cleansing power of the Holy Spirit every day of their lives as they submit to the Lordship of Christ Jesus.

Spouses will learn to become more patient and compassionate with each other as they model these attributes in their relationship, but change starts in the heart of each spouse individually before it happens in their relationship.

An exchange of attitudes and behavior is necessary to restore a marriage to health and wholeness. Spouses must exchange damaging (self-centered) behavior or negative attitudes for positive mindsets and humble (Christ-centered) behavior that reestablishes and/or restores love, trust and respect to their relationship. Here are some examples of positive exchanges:

| Infidelity | *exchanged for* | Fidelity |
| Rage | *exchanged for* | Peace/gentleness |
| Control | *exchanged for* | Humility |
| Fear | *exchanged for* | Faith |
| Anxiety | *exchanged for* | Hope |
| Aggression | *exchanged for* | Assertiveness |
| Detachment | *exchanged for* | Commitment |
| Powerlessness | *exchanged for* | Strength in Christ |

### Discussion Questions

1. From the list above, what exchanges do you need to make?
2. Is there an exchange that you have been avoiding?

## Changing Unhealthy Behavior

Sometimes a spouse holds onto unhealthy behavior out of fear and becomes unwilling to release their "right" to act out in anger, jealousy or pride. The willingness to change is the first step toward restoration. Spiritual growth is very limited until spouses are willing to exchange unhealthy for healthy behaviors.

*Mark and Sherry are a loving couple. Over the last seven years, they have experienced many blessings from their marriage. However, recurring conflicts seem overwhelming to them.*

*Mark has a tendency to become angry and Sherry struggles with jealousy. He becomes angry whenever she purchases clothes for the family or miscellaneous items for the house. Sherry becomes jealous of his schedule. She feels that her choices are limited, while his schedule includes hobbies like fishing and playing softball on a city league team. Sherry would like to have more personal time, but the needs of the children always seem to come at the expense of her schedule. They struggled with some of these issues throughout their premarital relationship, but they had little concern that anger or jealousy would continue to affect their marriage.*

*Sherry and Mark are struggling to adjust from their personal preferences and unique personalities to form a shared identity. They are learning that a shared identity requires them to consider each other's preferences and needs as equal to their own.*

Many couples believe that struggling with anger or jealousy will be easily resolved after they are married. Most couples are somewhat naïve in thinking that their spouse will be easily convinced by their logic or ways of doing things.

## Owning Your Sin

*Whenever Mark refuses to own his anger, Sherry is left trying to bear up under the weight of condemnation and judgment. Sherry can become angry like anyone else, but anger is not a bent that she struggles with regularly. Whenever Mark refuses to own his anger, Sherry becomes exasperated.*

*Sherry's negative bent is jealousy. She has learned to confess and repent of this sin and now works to protect her marriage from being consumed by jealousy. But if she is unwilling to acknowledge her jealous behavior, Mark is left to try to carry the consequences of unresolved jealousy.*

Spouses who are left to carry the burden of each other's negative bent will struggle to deescalate emotions that seem overwhelming to them. Couples who own their sinful bent will protect their spouse from having to bear up under the consequences of unconfessed sin. The following table will help couples to seek the Lord in regards to their sin patterns or being sinned against.

| Offended Spouse | Offending Spouse |
|---|---|
| Be willing to acknowledge that God's forgiveness is available to your spouse regardless of any desire that you have for retribution. | Accept that you have responsibility for sinful choices, regardless of any circumstances in your marriage. |
| Be willing to forgive your spouse by extending the same measure of grace to him/her that God has given you. | Forgive your spouse for any wrong that he/she has done, including hurtful responses to your sinful behavior. |
| Identify your losses and walk through the loss and grief cycle, learning how to grieve in a healthy way. | Resist the impulse to avoid the consequences of your sin. |
| God's faithfulness is not diminished through your marriage crisis. God will give you strength and hope for a better future. | Stop all unhealthy behavior and any contact with others that makes your spouse uncomfortable. |
| Be willing to rebuild trust with your spouse. | Submit to your spouse's need for honesty. |

| Offended Spouse | Offending Spouse |
| --- | --- |
| Acknowledging your need to receive healing and support for being sinned against. | Submit to any church discipline, establish healthy boundaries and be accountable to your spouse. |
| Acknowledge your need for personal and spiritual growth. | Take responsibility to follow biblical counsel for restoration. |

# CHAPTER FOURTEEN

# Reconciling a Crisis Marriage

## The Journey Back to Oneness

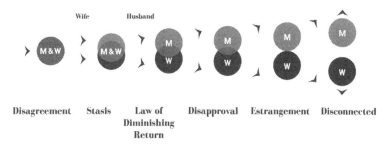

Regression from Oneness Model

The diagram above shows where the husband and wife are positioned in the Regression from Oneness. The wife has moved into Stage II (Stasis) and the husband is positioned at Stage III (Law of Diminished Return). At this point, the wife needs to reestablish the characteristics of commitment, intimacy and passion (physical intimacy) with her husband.

A couple cannot begin to restore physical intimacy by demanding sex from his/her spouse. They need to reestablish the emotional intimacy and commitment before physical intimacy is restored in their relationship. Spouses need to demonstrate faithfulness, and honor any boundaries that are needed to restore trust. Sexual intimacy does not make couples closer. Physical intimacy is a celebration of trust, fidelity and commitment. In order to restore these characteristics to their relationship, the wife needs to ask the husband:

- "What does it mean to share your heart with me?"
- "In what ways can I share my heart with you?"
- "What type of physical touch are you willing to receive from me?"

Physical intimacy never stands alone in the marriage relationship. Sexual intimacy benefits from each of the seventeen other characteristics in the Journey to Oneness in the diagram below:

**Identity**

**Friendship**

**Committed Dating**

**Engagement**

**Marriage Only**

**Blessing**

**Characteristics of the Six Stages**

Sex is a gift to give, as well as a gift to receive between a husband and wife. The wife needs her husband to be patient and understanding as she attempts to restore sexual intimacy between them.

The husband identifies with Stage III (Law of Diminished Return). He is responsible to reestablish the characteristics of responsibility, emotional honesty and a shared spiritual life with his wife. His wife needs to be encouraging and receptive as he initiates conversations with her. In order to restore these characteristics to the relationship and assure his wife that her needs are important to him, he needs to ask her:

- "In what ways can I demonstrate responsibility to you?"
- "Would you be willing to pray and read the Scriptures together?"
- "What questions do you want to ask me? I will answer you honestly."

A couple needs to be aware that his/her spouse may not be in a place to respond to all of these requests. They may be open to one or two, but not the third, and should accept any openness as a step toward restoring these areas of the relationship. A spouse needs to be slow to judge his/her struggling partner if they are unable to engage with every request for restoration. In so many cases, they have become paralyzed emotionally and spiritually due to the sin patterns in the offending spouse's life. Remember that God is patient. Additional healing or counsel may be required before a spouse can accept this invitation. Healing of the heart needs to start before restoration can take root. The future will be better than the past, but couples who find themselves in these stages must be responsible to change any behavior that has broken trust and crossed boundaries.

I have talked a lot about independence, but enmeshment or codependence is just as unhealthy when forming a shared identity. Someone who struggles with enmeshment (codependence) will blame him/herself for their spouse's poor behavior. This type of person will feel responsible to heal their relationship by becoming more submissive, compliant or sacrificial in order to turn things in a positive direction. Enmeshment creates an imbalance in mutuality between spouses who are equally responsible to receive and extend grace and mercy to one another. Perhaps two of the most common outcomes of enmeshed/codependent relationships are:

1. One spouse blames his/her behavior on their wife/husband's sinful choices.
2. An offended spouse minimizes the offending spouse's responsibility for breaking trust.

## Pathways to Reconciliation

Reconciliation begins when couples choose against the option of pursuing a divorce, even if the Scriptures support such action. Couples who embrace the hope of a reconciled marriage choose to stop the slide of regression and begin to listen for a word from God. Reconciliation is a spiritual journey, and the Holy Spirit will be your Guide and Counselor.

The following testimony reveals the tipping point that began the process of reconciliation for Jim and Sandy.

### The Power of Forgiveness

*Jim was totally unprepared for what his wife was about to disclose to him. Sandy made a confession of infidelity. While on a business trip, she made the biggest mistake of her life. For quite some time, their careers and financial goals received more attention than their relationship. Jim and Sandy's ambitions opened the door for a crisis in their marriage.*

*Sandy and Jim truly loved each other and neither one had ever suspected their spouse of being unfaithful or dissatisfied with their marriage. Fortunately, they went directly to their church and began* to meet with a pastor. Sandy wept with deep regret as Jim wept in disbelief. As she repented of her sin, they fell into each other's arms.

I asked Jim, "What did God place in your heart that allowed you to forgive Sandy and pursue reconciliation with her?"

He responded, "I didn't want Satan to ruin my family. I know that my wife made a terrible mistake, but we love each other deeply. Somehow we allowed our financial goals to come before our relationship. Both of us have to take responsibility for allowing our relationship to slip so far down on our list of priorities. Sandy fell into a trap that the enemy had set up to destroy her and our family.

"Our marriage was based on our faith, family and dreams of financial security. We wanted to be able to serve others as our business prospered. The core of our marriage was based on something more than a commitment to sexual fidelity."

As Jim looked back over the last few years, he realized that their priorities were working against them. He continued explaining, "We needed to own our mistakes and begin to rebuild our lives. My wife failed to honor one of our values, but she was faithful to fulfill all of the other commitments that we made to each other. Both of us made lifetime commitments to our marriage and family. I was determined to rebuild our relationship on my belief that our marriage was based on covenant rather than a civil contract. We were involved in a heavenly covenant and we stood on the promises that God would meet all of our needs according to his riches and glory. We were resolved to overcome the attack on our relationship."

I will never forget these words. Jim didn't want to let the enemy destroy his marriage.

I asked Sandy the same question.

She responded, "I was overwhelmed by the forgiveness and grace that God and my husband had extended toward me. My husband made me feel safe enough to deal with my sin and the guilt that gripped my soul. It was very difficult to stay focused on our reconciliation.

*Whenever I watched television or listened to a song on the radio, there seemed to be some reference to infidelity. I was constantly reminded of my sins and the pain that I brought on my family. I learned how the power of forgiveness could pull me through all of the shame and guilt that constantly filled my soul. There were many days that I had to simply fall into the arms of my husband and be reassured of his love for me.*

*"I am glad to report that our relationship is better than it has ever been and we are a restored couple. We just celebrated six years of a reconciled marriage."*

Thankfully, Sandy disclosed her sin to her husband and opened the door for reconciliation. Disclosure is always better than discovery.

## Disclosure and Discovery

Disclosure and discovery require different pathways toward reconciliation.

- *Disclosure* means that a spouse confesses, repents and seeks forgiveness from their husband/wife.
- *Discovery* means that a spouse is caught in his/her sinful and deceptive behavior.

Disclosure allows the offending spouse to approach their husband/wife in humility and obedience to the Lord as they confess their sins and deception for the sake of reconciliation.

Discovery is about exposing sinful behavior. One spouse is focused on exposing sin, while their husband/wife is trying to do damage control. For the most part, a spouse who has been caught in long-term patterns of sinful and self-centered behavior no longer recognizes what is true and righteous. At the time of discovery, the offending and offended spouses are both in crisis, and neither one of them is prepared to respond to the other out of grace and truth.

In some cases, the disclosing spouse perceives their sins as being far behind them. They feel that these areas of broken trust occurred in a different lifetime or that he/she has closed the book on sinful behavior. Unfortunately, their spouse is beginning on page one of a long novel.

An offended spouse may respond to the offending spouse's disclosure of sinful behavior as if these were happening currently. Because, for them, the pain and disappointment are real and overwhelming.

Couples are encouraged to know that disclosure is better than discovery and creates new opportunities to reestablish their relationship on the truth. In the big picture of reconciliation, it makes no difference how the truth came out. Truth makes a new beginning possible.

## Guiding Principles for Disclosure

| Healthy | Unhealthy |
|---------|-----------|
| Disclosure allows spouses to set boundaries that promote respect and responsibility between them. | Driven to know details of encounters, conversations and places. |
| Disclosure sets the tone for truth and reconciliation for the relationships. Blanket statements of forgiveness are not effective or lasting. | Driven to see a certain level of emotional pain or regret expressed by the offender. |
| Disclosure allows the offending spouse to respond to the victim's needs to establish boundaries with requests for counseling, etc. | Unwillingness to forgive before everything is disclosed. (In many cases, an offender is so trapped in deceit that he/she is unable to be honest for many months.) |

| Healthy | Unhealthy |
|---------|-----------|
| Disclosure allows spouses to move forward with honesty and openness. | Focuses on the past at the expense of dealing with the present. (You are a family that needs income, stability and active parenting.) |
| Disclosure allows spouses to identify any non-negotiable behavior in order to build new foundations of trust, such as:<br><br>• I can't have alcohol in our home.<br>• I can't be comfortable with you participating in social media.<br>• No more drinking or visiting bars.<br>• No private lunches with someone of the opposite sex. | Driven to prove someone to be a liar and judging them. |

Typically, the unsuspecting spouse will struggle with resentment when there is deception and withholding of the truth. This feeling may escalate if the offending spouse repeatedly denies any suspicions. Sometimes, the offending spouse tries to convince their spouse that they are imagining things or even "losing their mind" for suspecting anything. If this happens, he/she will feel indignant: "I knew something was going on! How could they lie to my face?"

Disclosure initiates a new beginning as well as a process. The offended spouse needs to focus on the entire pattern of deception rather than on specific incidents to be forgiven in the initial meeting of disclosure. Following the spouse's confession, repentance, willingness to submit to boundaries and counsel, there may be specific instances of deception that need to be fully disclosed. A spouse cannot forgive what he/she does not know, and an offending spouse cannot repent for what is undisclosed.

The couple should seek the help of a pastor or counselor before disclosing the sin(s) to one another. The offending spouse might also invite their husband/wife to go along with them to a meeting like Alcoholics Anonymous or a support group, or work together to install software to block porn sites, etc.

### The Voice of the Spirit

*Susan cried out, "God, if I don't hear something from you, I'm getting out of this marriage!"*

*Susan had a tendency to run from things in her life that were painful. The pain of her husband choosing another woman sent her reeling into the depths of her greatest fears. The discovery of Bill's infidelity also triggered some of her earliest childhood memories, which were filled with feelings of rejection from the people she loved the most. She wondered, "How could this be happening to me? I thought I had found my knight in shining armor."*

*The intensity of their pain and disappointment led them to consider looking for help from a source they had not considered relevant to their lives previously. They began attending a church in order to seek guidance in hope of finding healing for their lives and relationship.*

*Unfortunately, the first attempt at church didn't work well for them. The people were friendly and caring, but Bill and Susan didn't understand the religious expressions in the message or the worship. Their souls were screaming out in pain, but because everyone around them seemed so happy, they didn't want to unload their pain on this group of people. The second attempt at church changed everything for them. It was the church bulletin at Vineyard Columbus that opened a*

*door of hope for them. It read: "God wants to restore your marriage."
This was what they needed!*

*Bill and Susan immediately signed up for Begin Again, a ministry
that pairs crisis couples with couples who have restored their marriage. The Begin Again weekend and the six-week follow-up sessions
are designed to give couples hope, encouragement and support in their
journey of restoration. Couples in crisis do not have to stand alone.
They can stand side by side with couples who have experienced the
same pain and have learned to trust God and the church's ministry of
reconciliation.*

*By participating in Begin Again, Bill learned to confess and repent
of his sinful behavior and walk in a trustworthy manner. He was able
to listen to the counsel from other men who had fallen into the same
sinful patterns, but who now walked in holiness and humility.*

*Do you remember the cry of Susan's heart at the beginning of her
struggles? She had said: "God, if I don't hear something from you, I am
getting out of this marriage."*

*Bill and Susan had been walking in the pathway of reconciliation
for about six months when Susan received a letter from a woman
claiming to have had an affair with her husband. As she opened it,
these words jumped off the page: "Your husband is having an affair."
Immediately, all of her strength drained out of her soul. She thought
they had come so far, but now this was happening again.*

*Susan's newfound faith had become her anchor in the midst of this
severe storm. Sunday morning couldn't have arrived soon enough for
her. She came to church hoping to receive a word, a sign – anything –
from God about her marriage.*

*As Susan walked her daughter to Sunday school, she kept asking,
"Mommy, can I tell you my memory verse?" but Susan was so distracted by the contents of the letter that she couldn't fully comprehend
what her daughter was really asking. Finally, she responded, "Yes,
please tell me your verse."*

*And her daughter began quoting 1 Corinthians 13: "Love is patient, love is kind, it does not envy ... It keeps no record of wrongs ..."*

*At that moment, Susan heard the voice of the Spirit. Even though the letter served as a record of wrongs that her husband had committed, that morning she was able to let go of all the wrongs and embrace what was right about their relationship. Susan was able to hold to the course of reconciliation as her daughter recited 1 Corinthians 13.*

*Turns out, the information in the letter actually had been confessed early on in the restoration process. It was another attempt by the enemy of their souls and a woman who wanted to see their marriage destroyed. Susan needed to hear from God, and she received an answer to her prayers.*

Since that moment, Bill and Susan have celebrated ten years of reconciliation. They have become one of the bravest and most faithful couples that I have ever met.

### Digging out of Debt

*Kate and Tom were committed to get what they wanted out of life. Neither ever settled for anything less. Both of them wanted to get married and start a family, but it was much easier for them to move in together. Neither of them had considered making any concessions in their career goals or personal schedules before diving into their relationship but, after dating for more than five years, Tom gave Kate an ultimatum: "Marry me now or we're through." She agreed and they were married that same week.*

*Tom and Kate quickly became disillusioned with their relationship. Tom thought that getting married would be the catalyst that would allow them to draw close to each other but, unfortunately, they didn't know how to become interdependent. Kate began to look for ways to fill the void in her heart. She found that buying things gave her an escape from a now chaotic and demanding marriage.*

Tom started a new career. He needed to work long hours and had a rotating schedule that kept him from paying attention to the family budget. Meanwhile, Kate was getting very good at hiding her out-of-control spending habits. Her credit card debt climbed to $15,000, then to $25,000, and eventually beyond $40,000. She could no longer screen all the mail and calls from creditors. As the spending escalated, so did the physical and emotional abuse in their marriage. Trust was at an all-time low in their relationship when they finally decided to seek help.

Tom and Kate decided to attend a church to see if it would help. One Sunday morning, they listened as a guest speaker presented the Gospel. They both responded and turned their lives over to God. This was an important decision, but Tom and Kate were still looking for something to reverse the pattern of destructive behavior that was eating away at their commitment to one another.

God intervened. He heard their cry for help. He filled their hearts with a spirit of love and forgiveness. Their newfound faith allowed them to forge a new kind of partnership in their marriage. Faith and love quickly spilled over into their relationship and, for the first time, they began to face their troubles together. Without a strong spiritual compass, they had developed a value system that was based on taking care of "number one". They didn't know of any other way to live their lives. Marriages will not thrive when each person is only focused on what is best for them rather than the relationship.

Sacrificial love empowers couples to change self-centered behavior in order to serve one another in humility and faithfulness. Accountability is what pulled Kate beyond her guilt about her destructive spending habits. She began to face each late notice of an outstanding debt with honesty and integrity. She knew she couldn't go to a store alone, because the pull to make another purchase was so strong. Tom stood in the gap for his wife. He took the responsibility for the shopping in order to keep her from falling into temptation to buy items the *family didn't need.*

*As Tom learned to address his anger, he was able to create a safe haven for his wife. God transformed their lives as they confessed and repented of their sins. Obedience to the Scriptures helped them develop a budget and debt-reduction plan. They were able to pay off the entire debt but, even more, they had become rich in love, forgiveness and emotional honesty. No longer did they stand alone in their weakness.*

*Today, Tom and Kate are partners in life and faith. They asked God to save their marriage, and he offered them eternal life.*

Couples who put their faith in Jesus can reconcile their marriages. Marriage is a lifelong commitment that can become very challenging. Some spouses will experience the shock of sin that leads to disjointed marriages. Others will struggle with the slow burn of detached relationships. But there is hope!

Reconciliation is in the very breath of God. If you ask for his help, he will give you a word or image that will guide you onto the pathway of reconciliation. His presence can sustain any couple through any circumstance that threatens the restoration of their relationship. Jesus has promised to be with us. Reconciliation is his plan for every crisis marriage.

## Next Steps

My prayer is that your life and marriage will be filled with hope, peace, joy and reconciliation.

You can find blogs, resources and encouragement on the Life In Motion Resources™ web site at: lifeinmotionresources.com.

# Appendices

# Sample Strength
# Worksheet – Growing Friendship

## Agreement – Strength

| Woman | Man | Statement |
|-------|-----|-----------|
| A | A | My fiancé and I have a growing friendship. |

Woman agrees with: "My future husband and I have a growing friendship."

Man agrees with: "My future wife and I have a growing friendship."

## Scripture

Please meditate on the Scripture below for two days, then answer the following questions.

Song of Solomon 6:10: *"Who is this that appears like the dawn, fair as the moon, bright as the sun, majestic as the stars in procession?"*

## Participants: Woman & Man

What key words or phrases in this Scripture are relevant to you and your relationship with your future spouse?

## Participants: Man & Woman

How can this Scripture apply to the statement: "My fiancé and I have a growing friendship"?

> Proverbs 17:9 NKJV: *"He who covers over an offense promotes love, but whoever repeats the matter separates close friends."*

## Participants: Woman & Man

What key words or phrases in this Scripture are relevant to you and your relationship with your future spouse?

## Participants: Man & Woman

How can this Scripture apply to the statement: "My fiancé and I have a growing friendship"?

## Principles

1. Couples who choose to see and believe the best about each other will protect their relationship from becoming problem-focused.
2. Couples who commit to not being easily offended will maintain a vibrant relationship.
3. Couples who assume that they are loved do not withhold love and attention from their fiancé. Their relationship is based on mutual respect and honor.
4. Couples who presuppose that they are loved will not require their fiancé to prove or affirm their love in a demanding or suspicious way.

## Participants: Woman & Man

Select the principle that is most relevant to you.

## Participants: Man & Woman

How does this principle apply to your life and relationship with your future spouse?

### Participants: Man & Coach

How does this principle apply to your life and relationship with your future spouse?

## Couple's Worksheet Section (to be completed together)

### Woman's Strength Questions
### Participants: Woman, Man, Coach

Woman asks Man: "What type of activities help our friendship to mature?"

Give one or two examples.

### Man's Strength Questions
### Participants: Woman, Man, Coach

Man asks Woman: "What type of activities help our friendship to mature?"

Give one or two examples.

# Engaged/Seriously Dating
# Couple's Assessment

This assessment is for engaged or seriously dating couples that are talking about marriage in their future. (Married couples may skip ahead.) The couple completes the self-assessments in each relationship category by marking each statement with a plus (+) or minus (-) sign. The assessment will allow engaged couples to see how their relationship compares to others who report high couple satisfaction in these same areas.

Premarital couples have these six areas in common:

1. Relational maturity
2. Relational validation
3. Proactive conflict management
4. Personal and family boundaries
5. Emotional maturity
6. Shared spiritual life

Dating couples will need to replace fiancé with boy/girlfriend.

1. Relational Maturity

   The relational maturity assessment is made up of twenty-one statements. Couples who report satisfaction in the area of relational maturity have these statements in common. The table below represents a partial list of the statements associated with relational maturity. Scriptures are included to show correlations between the statements and biblical values.

| +/- | Relational Maturity |
|-----|---------------------|
| | • I am empathetic when my fiancé is overwhelmed (Ephesians 4:32). |
| | • My fiancé is empathetic when I am overwhelmed. |
| | • I regularly use encouraging words when I talk to my fiancé (Ephesians 4:29). |
| | • My fiancé regularly uses encouraging words when he/she talks to me. |
| | • I am quick to forgive my fiancé (Colossians 3:13–14). |
| | • My fiancé is quick to forgive me. |
| | • I am accountable to another Christian other than my fiancé (Proverbs 27:17). |
| | • My fiancé is accountable to another Christian other than me. |
| | • I express my affection to my fiancé with words (Song of Solomon 1:9–10, 16). |
| | • My fiancé expresses his/her affection to me with words. |
| | • I balance work and home responsibilities well. |
| | • My fiancé balances work and home responsibilities well. |

2. Relational Validation

Engaged couples reporting satisfaction in the area of relational validation have these statements in common. Couples who value mutuality and respect and speak well of each other will benefit from positive affirmation and encouragement. The table below represents a partial list of the fifteen factors that describe relational validation.

| +/- | Relational Validation |
|---|---|
| | • I do not speak poorly of my spouse to friends and/or family (1 Corinthians 13:4–6). |
| | • My fiancé does not speak poorly of me to friends and/or family. |
| | • I treat my fiancé as an equal partner (Galatians 3:28). |
| | • I often ask my fiancé for his/her opinion (Proverbs 1:5; 12:15). |
| | • My fiancé often asks me for my opinion. |
| | • I am respectful of my fiancé's ideas (Proverbs 3:7–8; 19:20). |
| | • My fiancé is respectful of my ideas. |
| | • My leisure activities negatively affect our relationship.* |
| | • My fiancé's leisure activities negatively affect our relationship.* |
| | *Indicates a negative statement – couples disagree with this statement. |

3. Proactive Conflict Resolution

Engaged couples reporting couple satisfaction in the area of conflict resolution have these statements in common. These statements show an absence of passive-aggressive behavior, anger, conflict avoidance, becoming silent when misunderstood or a need for unusual closeness in the relationship. The table below represents a partial list of the factors associated with proactive conflict resolution.

| +/- | Proactive Conflict Management |
|-----|-------------------------------|
| | • I am not passive-aggressive with my anger toward my spouse (Hebrews 12:14–15).* <br> • My fiancé is passive-aggressive when angry with me.* <br> • I avoid conflict with my spouse (Romans 12:18).* <br> • My fiancé avoids conflict with me.* <br> *Indicates that couples disagree with this statement.* |

4. Personal and Family Boundaries

   Engaged couples reporting satisfaction in the areas of personal and family boundaries have these statements in common. These statements reveal a commitment to financial responsibility and healthy boundaries with family members, coworkers and friends. The table below represents a partial list of the factors associated with personal and family boundaries.

| +/- | Personal and Family Boundaries |
|-----|-------------------------------|
| | • I stay within our budget plan (Proverbs 9:13). <br> • My fiancé stays with his/her budget plan. <br> • My extended family's involvement in our lives is appropriate. <br> • My fiancé's extended family's involvement in our lives is appropriate. <br> • I allow others to take advantage of me. <br> • My fiancé does not allow others to take advantage of him/her. |

5. Emotional Maturity

   Engaged couples reporting satisfaction in the area of emotional maturity have these statements in common. Emotional maturity can be described as self-awareness. Emotionally mature persons are aware of negative feelings that are being expressed during conflict, misunderstandings or crisis. An emotionally mature person is able to extend the characteristics of peace, empathy and forgiveness to their fiancé as needed.

| +/- | Emotional Maturity |
|-----|--------------------|
| | • I am empathetic when my fiancé is overwhelmed.<br>• My fiancé is empathetic when I am overwhelmed.<br>• I am quick to forgive my fiancé.<br>• My fiancé is quick to forgive me.<br>• I am bitter toward my fiancé.*<br>*Indicates that couples disagree with this statement.* |

6. Shared Spiritual Life

Engaged couples reporting satisfaction in the area of their shared spiritual life have these statements in common. As couples develop a shared spiritual life, they will learn how God works uniquely in each person. Couples who share spiritual insights, pray for one another, serve together and develop friendships with other Christians will find deeper levels of trust in their relationship.

| +/- | Shared Spiritual Life |
|-----|------------------------|
| | • I often ask my fiancé to pray for me (1 Thessalonians 5:16).<br>• I am accountable to another Christian other than my fiancé (Proverbs 27:17).<br>• I regularly share spiritual insights with my fiancé (2 Timothy 2:15).<br>• My fiancé regularly shares spiritual insights with me. |

Identify one or two of the statements in each relationship category that you marked with a minus sign. As you read this book, you will find resources and practical applications to turn these minus signs into plus signs.

# Married Couple's Assessment

This assessment is only for married couples. The couple completes the self-assessments in each relationship category by marking each statement with a plus (+) or minus (-) sign. This assessment will allow married couples to see how their relationships compare to others who report couple satisfaction in the following areas:

1. Relational maturity
2. Differentiation
3. Healthy boundaries
4. Mutuality
5. Parenting values
6. Proactive conflict resolution
7. Sexual compatibility

1. Relational Maturity

   Couples who report satisfaction in the area of relational maturity have nineteen statements in common. Relational maturity is characterized by harmony and closeness. The table below represents only a partial list of these statements. Scriptures are included to show correlations between the statements and biblical values.

| +/- | Relational Maturity |
|-----|---------------------|
| | • I regularly use encouraging words when I talk to my spouse (Ephesians 4:29–32). |
| | • I am a good listener (James 1:9). |
| | • I focus on my spouse's positive characteristics (Philippians 2:14–15). |
| | • I repent quickly when I am wrong (James 5:16). |
| | • I am quick to forgive my spouse (Colossians 3:13–14). |
| | • I am willing to defer to my spouse when we can't come to an agreement (Philippians 2:4). |

2. Relational Differentiation

Couples who report satisfaction in the area of relational differentiation have twelve statements in common. Relational differentiation includes positivity, mutuality, faith, interdependence and humility. The table below represents a partial list of these twelve statements.

| +/- | Relational Differentiation |
|-----|----------------------------|
| | • I resolve conflicts with my spouse quickly (Hebrews 12:14). |
| | • I am consistent with how I resolve conflicts with my spouse (Proverbs 11:3). |
| | • I am able to talk with my spouse about things that we disagree on (Ephesians 5:25–26). |
| | • I am good at expressing my negative feelings to my spouse (Proverbs 27:5–6). |
| | • I am quick to identify the problem(s) that lead to conflict with my spouse. |
| | • I alienate my spouse when we have a conflict.* |
| | *Indicates that couples disagree with this statement.* |

3.  Healthy Boundaries

    Couples reporting satisfaction in the area of healthy bounda-
    ries have ten statements in common. Boundaries are essential in
    all healthy relationships. These types of boundaries ensure that
    couples or family members demonstrate respect and humility by
    allowing one another to finish their statements before respond-
    ing. They consider each other to be coequals in the relationship.
    The statements in the table below represent only a partial list of
    the ten statements.

| +/- | Healthy Boundaries |
|-----|--------------------|
|     | • I treat my spouse as a coequal (Galatians 3:28). <br> • I treat my spouse as an equal partner (Ephesians 5:21). <br> • I listen to my spouse's point of view when we disagree (James 3:17). <br> • I balance work and home responsibilities well. |

4.  Mutuality

    Couples who report satisfaction in the area of mutuality have
    eleven statements in common. Mutuality promotes validation
    and interdependence in marriage relationships. Communication
    and conflict resolution skills are strengths among these couples.
    The statements below represent a partial list of these statements.

| +/- | Mutuality |
|-----|-----------|
| | • I am quick to forgive my spouse (Proverbs 17:9). |
| | • I treat my spouse as a coequal (Ephesians 5:21). |
| | • I share the leadership of our family equally with my spouse (Mark 9:35). |
| | • I am able to talk with my spouse about things that we disagree on (Ephesians 5:25–26). |
| | • I listen to my spouse's point of view when we disagree (James 3:17). |
| | • I resolve conflicts with my spouse quickly (Hebrews 12:14). |

5.  Parenting Values

    Couples reporting satisfaction in the area of parenting values have nine statements in common. These statements reveal that affection, faith, respect and shared parenting values are necessary elements of couple satisfaction. The statements in the table below represent a partial list of these characteristics.

| +/- | Parenting Values |
|-----|------------------|
| | • I am supportive of my spouse's parenting values, i.e. honesty, integrity, and faith. |
| | • I show affection to the children (Matthew 18:10–11). |
| | • Our children respond well to my affection and initiative toward them (Matthew 19:13–14). |
| | • I spend an appropriate amount of quality time with our children. |

6.  Proactive Conflict Resolution

    Couples reporting satisfaction in the area of conflict resolution have four statements in common. These statements show an absence of passive-aggressive behavior.

| +/- | Proactive Conflict Resolution |
|-----|-------------------------------|
|     | • I am good at expressing my negative feelings to my spouse (Proverbs 27:5–6). <br> • I want peace with my spouse at any cost (Romans 12:18).* <br> • I become silent when my spouse doesn't understand me (Ecclesiastes 3:7).* <br> *Indicates that couples disagree with this statement.* |

7. Sexual Compatibility

Couples reporting relationship satisfaction in the area of sexual compatibility have three statements in common. Friendship is a key element in forming sexual compatibility. Friends talk and learn how to put themselves in each other's circumstances in order to be supportive and encouraging.

| +/- | Sexual Compatibility |
|-----|----------------------|
|     | • I am content with the intimacy level of our sexual relationship (Song of Solomon 6:3). <br> • I need more closeness in our marriage.* <br> *Indicates that couples disagree with this statement.* |

Now identify one or two of the statements in each relationship category that you marked with a minus sign. You are now ready to start your Journey to Oneness.

It is my intention that, as you read this book, these minus signs will turn into plus signs if you are thinking about your marriage. There are no shortcuts on this journey. My prayer is that you will be empowered as a couple to overcome all the ups and downs of life.

After all my years of pastoring couples, I am confident that this Journey to Oneness is worth the time and attention required to enrich your relationship.

# Worksheet –
# Supportive of Dreams and Goals

## Agreement – Strength

| Woman | Man | Statement |
|-------|-----|-----------|
| A (A) | A (A) | I support the dreams and goals of my fiancé. |

Woman agrees with: "I support the dreams and goals of my future husband."

Man agrees with: "I support the dreams and goals of my future wife."

Man agrees with: "My future wife is supportive of my dreams and goals."

Woman agrees with: "My future husband is supportive of my dreams and goals."

## Scripture

Please meditate on the Scripture below for two days, then answer the following questions.

Amos 3:3: *"Do two walk together unless they have agreed to do so?"*

## Participants: Woman & Man

What key words or phrases in this Scripture are relevant to you and your relationship with your future spouse?

## Participants: Man & Woman

How can this Scripture apply to the statement: "I support the dreams and goals of my future spouse"?

> Jeremiah 29:11: *"'For I know the plans I have for you,' declares the LORD, 'plans to prosper you and not to harm you, plans to give you hope and a future.'"*

## Participants: Woman & Man

What key words or phrases in this Scripture are relevant to you and your relationship with your future spouse?

## Participants: Man & Woman

How can this Scripture apply to the statement: "I support the dreams and goals of my future spouse"?

## Principles

1. Couples are uniquely gifted to help each other fulfill God's plans for their life.
2. One person must not pursue her/his dream or goal at the expense of her/his future spouse.
3. Couples who support each other's dreams will develop deep levels of trust and respect for each other.

## Participants: Woman & Man

Select the principle that is most relevant to you.

## Participants: Man & Woman

How does this principle apply to your life and relationship with your future spouse?

## Couple's Worksheet Section (to be completed together)

### Woman's Strength Questions
### Participants: Woman & Man

Woman asks Man: "How do I demonstrate that I am supportive of your dreams and goals?"

Give one or two examples.

### Man's Strength Questions
### Participants: Man & Woman

Man asks Woman: "How do I demonstrate that I am supportive of your dreams and goals?"

Give one or two examples.

# Indicators of a Healthy
# or Unhealthy Relationship

Engaged or dating couples will need to replaces the word "spouse" with "fiancé/fiancée" or "boy/girlfriend". Place a plus sign (+) next to the statements that frequently occur in your relationship. Place a minus sign (-) next to statements that occur infrequently in your relationship. Leave statements blank that never occur in your relationship. Place a double plus sign (++) next to any indicators on the unhealthy relationship side to indicate actions or behavior that cause you great concern.

It does not mean that, whenever a plus sign (+) is given to an unhealthy indicator, he/she is an abusive person. However, each person must be willing to change these types of behavior and demonstrate that they have broken this pattern. A professional counselor can be a great resource for couples/individuals who need to break these types of patterns and behavior.

## Instructions

Assess your own behavior as well as your fiancé/fiancée, boy/girlfriend or spouse's behavior over the last year.

| Healthy Indicator | | | Unhealthy Indicator | | |
|---|---|---|---|---|---|
| M | F | Mutual Respect | M | F | Demanding Respect |
| | | Listening without judging. | | | Demanding respect from your spouse. |
| | | Being emotionally affirming and understanding. | | | Displaying arrogance and superiority toward your spouse. |
| | | Valuing the other person's opinions even if these opinions are different from yours. | | | Demanding like-mindedness. |
| | | Supporting the other person's goals and dreams. | | | Diminished view of the other person's dreams/goals. |
| | | Serving one another with acts of kindness. | | | Using male/female privilege. Presenting oneself in a superior way. |
| M | F | Safety/Emotional Support | M | F | Violence/ Emotional Abuse |
| | | Talking and acting in a way that is nonthreatening. | | | Making threats to hurt spouse/children (physically or sexually); damaging property. |

| | | | | | |
|---|---|---|---|---|---|
| | | Emotional honesty – encourage your spouse to express negative feelings or emotions. | | | Criticizing your spouse – making them feel bad about themselves – character assassination. |
| | | Celebrating your unique identities. | | | Name calling, degrading or humiliating your spouse |
| | | Empathetic when your spouse is emotional without judgment or criticism. | | | Using jealousy, anger, etc. to justify abuse; blaming your spouse for your poor behavior. |
| **M** | **F** | **Collaboration** | **M** | **F** | **Control** |
| | | Seeking mutually acceptable resolutions to conflict. | | | Demanding your way as the only way. |
| | | Being flexible – willingness to adjust when something needs to change. | | | Threatening to leave or commit suicide. |
| | | Being willing to compromise. | | | Unwilling to compromise or accept changes. |
| | | Respect each other's opinions that may differ from your own. | | | Using looks, actions and gestures to intimidate in order to get your way. |

| M | F | Fostering Trust | M | F | Denial of Responsibility |
|---|---|---|---|---|---|
|   |   | Accepting personal responsibility for sinful behavior. |   |   | Minimizing and denying your sinful behavior. |
|   |   | Acknowledging your sinful behavior and willingness to repent. |   |   | Making light of your abusive behavior or blaming others for sinful actions. |
|   |   | Willingness to admit being wrong. |   |   | Minimizing your spouse's need for the truth. |
|   |   | Communicating openly and truthfully. |   |   | Shifting responsibility for abusive behavior (blaming). |
| **M** | **F** | **Mutual Submission** | **M** | **F** | **Subservience to Your Spouse** |
|   |   | Modeling submission to the Lord. |   |   | Requiring hierarchy in relationship (male/female bias). |
|   |   | Displaying servant leadership. |   |   | Treating spouse like a servant. |
|   |   | Making family decisions together. |   |   | Making all the big decisions alone. |

| | | | | | |
|---|---|---|---|---|---|
| | | Sharing parenting responsibilities. | | | Undermining the other parent to maintain "control" over children. |
| | | Mutual agreement on a fair distribution of household responsibilities. | | | Defining the roles and responsibilities for your partner. |
| | | Making financial decisions together. | | | Controlling money; making your spouse ask for money; requiring an accounting of every penny. |
| **M** | **F** | **Fidelity** | **M** | **F** | **Infidelity** |
| | | Honoring commitments/marriage covenant. | | | Adultery, pornography, emotional affairs. |
| | | Being faithful (in mind, heart and body). | | | Withholding emotional intimacy. |
| | | Fulfilling your responsibilities and promises. | | | Not fulfilling responsibilities and promises. |

| M | F | Communication | M | F | Secretive |
|---|---|---|---|---|---|
| | | Focus on potential solutions to conflict instead of problems. | | | Avoiding conflict/ accountability by changing the subject. |
| | | Displaying effective listening skills. | | | Ignoring and yelling to intimidate or get your way. |
| | | Acknowledging/ affirming. | | | Alienating your spouse with time away, job schedule, purchases and friendships. |
| | | Getting your point across in a respectful way. | | | Lying or keeping secrets to avoid responsibility/truth. |
| M | F | Self-sacrificing | M | F | Self-seeking |
| | | Encouraging your spouse to spend time with family and friends. | | | Demanding your spouse spends all their time with you. |
| | | Supporting your spouse's goals and dreams. | | | Limiting your spouse's outside interests and activities to your preferences. |

| M | F | Self-sacrificing | M | F | Self-seeking |
|---|---|---|---|---|---|
|  |  | Modeling patience/love (1 Cor. 13). |  |  | Displaying a sense of entitlement (sex, money, etc.). |
|  |  | Putting your spouse's wants and needs above your own. |  |  | Showing little or no concern for your spouse's wants and needs; expecting your needs to supersede everything else, including young children. |

# Worksheet – Patience

## Agreement – Improvement Needed

| Wife | Husband | Statement |
|------|---------|-----------|
| B (B) | C (C) | I am patient with my spouse. |

Husband disagrees with: "I am patient with my wife."
Wife agrees with: "I am patient with my husband."
Wife disagrees with: "My husband is patient with me."
Husband agrees with: "My wife is patient with me."

## Scripture

Please meditate on the Scripture below for two days, then answer the following questions.

> Galatians 5:22: *"But the fruit of the Spirit is love, joy, peace, patience, kindness, goodness, faithfulness, gentleness and self-control. Against such things there is no law."*

## Participants: Wife & Husband

What key words or phrases in this Scripture are relevant to you and your relationship with your spouse?

## Participants: Husband & Wife

How can this Scripture apply to the statement: "I am patient with my spouse"?

Proverbs 19:11: *"A person's wisdom gives him patience; it is to one's glory to overlook an offense."*

## Participants: Wife & Husband

What key words or phrases in this Scripture are relevant to you and your relationship with your spouse?

## Participants: Wife & Coach

How can this Scripture apply to the statement: "I am patient with my spouse"?

## Principles

1. Patience is a virtue – a godly attribute that creates hope and trust in a relationship.
2. God wants you to express greater measures of patience with others around you.

## Wife's response

Select the principle that is most relevant to you.

## Participants: Husband & Wife

Select the principle that is most relevant to you.

## Discussion Questions

1. Do you regularly pray to be more patient with your spouse?
2. Do you ask God to change you rather than asking God to change your spouse?

## Participants: Wife & Husband

How does this discussion question apply to your life and relationship with your spouse?

## Practical Application

## Participants: Husband & Wife

1. Make a list of the areas in your relationship that require you or your spouse to express more patience with each other.
2. Read the following meditation and discussion together. Pray blessings over each other using the prayer below.

### Patience

> Proverbs 15:18 (NIV): *"A hot-tempered person stirs up conflict, but the one who is patient calms a quarrel."*

> Proverbs 19:11 (NIV): *"A person's wisdom yields patience; it is to one's glory to overlook an offense."*

## Participants: Wife & Husband

With whom, or in what areas of your life, could you use an extra portion of patience?

## Participants: Husband & Wife

Discuss what these proverbs say about the benefits of being a patient person.

## Participants: Wife & Husband

How would being more patient benefit your relationship with your spouse and/or your children?

## Wife's Prayer for Husband

Father, thank you for _____ and for all the ways that he accepts my different views and ways of doing things. I ask that you would increase his ability to be patient with others. I pray that our home will be blessed by his ability to overlook offenses and model patience in the midst of quarrels. I ask that you would use him to demonstrate how patience overcomes conflicts in his relationship and work environment. Amen.

## Husband's Prayer for Wife

Father, thank you for _____ and for all the ways that she accepts my different views and ways of doing things. I ask that you would increase her ability to be patient with others. I pray that our home will be blessed by her ability to overlook offenses and model patience in the midst of quarrels. I ask that you would use her to demonstrate how patience overcomes conflicts in her relationship and work environment. Amen.[1]

# Couple's Worksheet Section (to be completed together)

## Husband's Improvement Questions
## Participants: Husband & Wife

Husband asks Wife: "Do I become impatient with you over specific subjects or circumstances?"
Husband asks Wife: "How can I make it better?"

Give one or two examples that are measurable, reasonable and repeatable.

## Wife's Strength Questions
## Participants: Wife & Husband

Wife asks Husband: "How do I demonstrate patience with you?"
Give one or two examples.

---

[1] Written by Mindy and Jason Layman.

# Worksheet – Praying with Each Other

Couples can begin to reestablish spiritual disciplines by completing their LIMRI Praying with Each Other Worksheet. Relationship status will determine if the worksheet reflects dating, engaged or married relationships.

## Agreement – Improvement Needed

| Wife | Husband | Statement |
|------|---------|-----------|
| C | C | We pray with each other on a regular basis. |

Wife disagrees with: "I pray with my husband on a regular basis."
Husband disagrees with: "I pray with my wife on a regular basis."

## Scripture

Please meditate on the Scripture below for two days, then answer the following questions.

Colossians 4:2: *"Devote yourselves to prayer, being watchful and thankful."*

## Participants: Husband & Wife

What key words or phrases in this Scripture are relevant to you and your relationship with your spouse?

## Participants: Husband & Wife

How can this Scripture apply to the statement: "We pray with each other on a regular basis"?

## Principles

1. Couples must learn to receive prayer from their spouse.
2. Couples that pray together will protect their relationship from the spiritual attack of Satan and the cultural lies that diminish the holiness of their relationship.
3. God will give you insight on how to pray for each other.
4. There are real enemies of your relationship and prayer will guard your relationship.
5. Couples that pray together develop a deep level of trust and respect for each other.

## Participants: Husband & Wife.

Select the principle that is most relevant to you.

## Participants: Husband & Wife

How does this principle apply to your life and relationship with your spouse?

## Discussion Questions

## Husband & Wife's responses

1. Do you initiate prayer with your spouse?
2. Are you willing to receive prayer from your spouse?
3. Can you talk openly to your spouse about areas where you struggle in order to receive prayer from them?

### Participants: Husband & Wife

Select the discussion question that was most relevant to you.

### Participants: Husband & Wife

How does this discussion question apply to your life and relationship with your spouse?

## Couple's Worksheet Section (to be completed together)

### Woman's Improvement Questions
### Participants: Husband & Wife

Wife asks Husband: "What is keeping you from praying with me on a regular basis?"

### Participants: Husband & Wife

Husband asks Wife: "How can I be more intentional in developing a shared prayer life with you?"

Give one or two examples that are measurable, reasonable and repeatable.

### Participants: Husband & Wife

How can these changes enhance our relationship?

### Husband's Improvement Questions

### Participants: Husband & Wife

Husband asks Wife: "What is keeping you from praying with me on a regular basis?"

### Participants: Husband & Wife

Wife asks Husband: "How can I be more intentional in developing a shared prayer life with you?"

Give one or two examples that are measurable, reasonable and repeatable.

## Participants: Husband & Wife

How can these changes enhance our relationship?

# Premarital Questionnaire

The following questionnaire will allow couples to identify areas of their past that have the potential to create a trust wound in their lives. Couples who want to move toward a marriage covenant will need to disclose their sexual history, past abuse, addictive behavior or trust wounds from former relationships.

## Sexual History

At least two-thirds of newly married couples say that the first year of their marriage required more adjustments than they had anticipated in their sexual relationship. Many couples are unprepared for the level of communication that it takes to develop a vibrant sexual relationship. Communication and trust are just as important as passion and desire between a husband and wife.

It is essential that engaged couples share their sexual history with each other. Couples must learn to embrace all of the history, choices and consequences that are associated with previous sexual activity. People should never enter into marriage before they have shared these details with their fiancé.

| | Childhood (0–14) | Adulthood | Recent (Within last year) |
|---|---|---|---|
| Illicit online communication/pictures | ☐ | ☐ | ☐ |
| Pornography | ☐ | ☐ | ☐ |
| Sexual abuse/Incest | ☐ | ☐ | ☐ |
| Rape | ☐ | ☐ | ☐ |
| Sexual activity outside of marriage | ☐ | ☐ | ☐ |
| STDs | ☐ | ☐ | ☐ |
| Homosexuality | ☐ | ☐ | ☐ |
| Soliciting/Prostitution | ☐ | ☐ | ☐ |
| Sexual addiction | ☐ | ☐ | ☐ |
| Abortion | ☐ | ☐ | ☐ |
| Miscarriage | ☐ | ☐ | ☐ |

# A Case of Divorce

Couples who receive counsel and exhaust every opportunity for reconciliation before they separate or divorce should never feel as if their character is being called into question. In many cases of divorce, a spouse is not given an opportunity to pursue reconciliation because their husband/wife refuses to stop sinful behavior and has developed a hardness of heart toward God and their marriage.

Divorce is never an isolated incident. Each divorce affects hundreds of people in their communities and churches. The following principles will help spouses to decide when divorce is the only option for their relationship:

### Principle 1 – Couples do not divorce in order to remarry someone else.

### Principle 2 – Divorce is not to be used as a pathway toward reconciliation.

- Some couples choose to end their marriage with the hope of creating a level playing field to start a new relationship with each other. They feel that a divorce will allow them to put an end to the controlling or unhealthy behavior that has developed in their relationship.

- Marriage is a sacred vow and should never be terminated for the abovementioned purposes. Spouses should do everything possible to avoid divorce by seeking pastoral counsel.

## Principle 3 – Divorce is a choice against reconciliation.

- The biblical guidelines that permit divorce include infidelity, abandonment, and committing the crime of domestic violence against one's spouse. The spouse who files for divorce/dissolution is making a choice against reconciliation. This choice should only be made after exhausting all avenues for reconciliation.

- Even though domestic violence is not specifically mentioned in the Bible as a guideline for divorce, it is contrary to every characteristic of loving relationships. Violence against one's spouse is a criminal act.

- Other covenant-breaking behavior includes: withholding conjugal love, financial irresponsibility and withholding emotional support (Exodus 21:10–11).

- Professional and pastoral counseling and marriage coaching are just a few of the resources that couples can use to restore their marriage.

## Principle 4 – Divorce should only be considered in conjunction with the counsel given by the leadership of the church the couple attends.

## Principle 5 – Divorce is primarily due to the hardness of heart of the spouse who has broken their marriage covenant vows. Hardness of heart is defined by an unwillingness to submit to God, the Scriptures, the counsel of the church, or their spouse. An offending spouse who refuses to submit to each of these areas has demonstrated hardness of heart. The spouse of the offender is free to pursue a divorce at their discretion.

# Bibliography

Balswick, J. O. (2014). *The Family*: *A Christian Perspective on the Contemporary Home*. Grand Rapids: Baker Books. Print.

BEFORE IT'S NEWS. (2013, June 17). "U.S. marriage rates are at historic lows." Retrieved from: www.beforeitsnews.com/native-american-news/2013/06/u-s-marriage-rates-are-at-historic-lows-2447928.html. Web.

Bramlett, M. D. and W. D. Mosher. (2001). "First marriage dissolution, divorce, and remarriage: United States." *Advance data from vital and health statistics 232*. Hyattsville: National Center for Health Statistics. Print.

Cherlin, Andrew. (2010). *The Marriage-Go-Round: The State of Marriage and the Family in America Today*. New York: Vintage Books. Print.

Glenn, N. D. (2005). "With This Ring …" *A National Survey on Marriage in America*. Gaithersburg: National Fatherhood Initiative.

Infoplease. (2000–2015). "Median Age at First Marriage, 1890–2010." Retrieved from: http://www.infoplease.com/ipa/A0005061.html. Web. 16 Nov. 2015.

Jayson, S. (2013, June 7). "Marriage rates may be low, but more weddings predicted." Retrieved from USA TODAY: http://www.usatoday.com/story/news/nation/2013/06/17/marriage-trends-demographics/2424641/. Web.

Jeon, J. K. (1999). *Covenant Theology*. Lanham: University Press of America. Print.

Johnston, S. (2013, July 13). "More Single Women Buying Homes Than Single Men." Retrieved from U.S. NEWS Money: http://money.usnews.com/money/personal-finance/

articles/2013/07/08/more-single-women-buying-homes-than-single-men. Web.

Kayser, K. and J. Johnson. (2008). "Divorce." Ed. T. Mizrahi and L. Davis. *Encyclopedia of Social Work.* Washington, DC: NASW Press. 76-85. Print.

Kilmann, K. W. (2009). "An Overview of the Thomas-Kilmann Conflict Mode Instrument (TKI)." Retrieved from TKI: http://www.kilmanndiagnostics.com/overview-thomas-kilmann-conflict-mode-instrument-tki. Web.

The Knot. (1997–2016). "Wedding Money: What Does the Average Wedding Cost?" Retrieved from: https://www.theknot.com/content/what-does-the-average-wedding-cost. Web.

Loehrke, J. (2013, June 13). "U.S. marriage rates are at historic lows but may soon rebound a bit, demographers predict." Retrieved from USA TODAY: http://www.usatoday.com/story/news/nation/2013/06/17/marriage-trends-demographics/2424641/. Web.

Mather, M. and D. Lavery. (Sept. 2010). "In U.S., Proportion Married at Lowest Recorded Levels." Population Reference Bureau. Prb.org. Web. 16 Nov. 2015.

Maxwell, J. (2004). *Relationships 101.* Nashville: Thomas Nelson. Print.

Merriam-Webster. (2011). "Ambivalence." Retrieved from: Merriam-Webster.com. Web. 2015.

Merriam-Webster. (2011). "Change." Retrieved from: Merriam-Webster.com. Web. 2015.

Merriam-Webster. (2011). "Engagement." Retrieved from: Merriam-Webster.com. Web. 2015.

Merriam-Webster. (2011). "Exclusive." Retrieved from: Merriam-Webster.com. Web. 2015.

Merriam-Webster. (2011). "Mediation." Retrieved from: Merriam-Webster.com. Web. 2015.

Merriam-Webster. (2011). "Validation." Retrieved from: Merriam-Webster.com. Web. 2015.

Miller, S. H. (2013, May 23). "The Seminary Gender Gap." Retrieved from: Christianitytoday.com:http://www.christianitytoday.com/women/2013/may/seminary-gender-gap.html. Web.

Perry, M. J. (2013, May 13). "Stunning college degree gap: Women have earned almost 10 million more college degrees than men since 1982." Retrieved from American Enterprise Institute: https://www.aei.org/publication/stunning-college-degree-gap-women-have-earned-almost-10-million-more-college-degrees-than-men-since-1982/. Web.

Safier, R. and W. Roberts. (2003). *There Goes the Bride: Making Up Your Mind, Calling it Off and Moving On.* San Francisco: Jossey-Bass. Print.

Sound Vision. (2015, July 25). "Wedding Statistics in the United States." Retrieved from: http://www.soundvision.com/article/wedding-statistics-in-the-united-states. Web.

*Spirit-Filled Life Bible: New King James Version.* (1991). Ed. J. W. Hayford. Nashville: Thomas Nelson Publishers. Print.

Thomas, Gary. (2000). *Sacred Marriage.* Grand Rapids: Zondervan. Print.

U.S. Department of Labor, Women's Bureau. (2011, January). "Women in the Labor Force in 2010." Retrieved from United States Department of Labor: http://www.dol.gov/wb/factsheets/Qf-laborforce-10.htm. Web.

Wikipedia. (2015). "*Lectio Divina.*" Retrieved from: https://en.wikipedia.org/wiki/Lectio_Divina. Web.

Wineberg, H. (1992). "Childbearing and dissolution of the second marriage." *Journal of Marriage and the Family* 54.4: 879-887. Print.

67962013R00126

Made in the USA
Columbia, SC
03 August 2019